AF265345

Person, Place, and World:
A Late-Modern Reading of Robert Frost

Steven Frattali

Person, Place, and World: A Late-Modern Reading of Robert Frost

English Literary Studies
University of Victoria
2002

© 2002 by Steven Frattali

ELS Editions
Department of English
University of Victoria
Victoria, BC
Canada V8W 3W1
www.elseditions.com

Founding Editor: Samuel L. Macey

General Editor: Luke Carson

Printed by CreateSpace

No part of this publication may be reproduced, stored in a retrieval system or transmitted, in any form or by any means. Without the prior written consent of the publisher or a licence from The Canadian Copyright Licensing Agency (Access Copyright). For an Access Copyright licence, visit *www.accesscopyright.ca* or call toll free to 1–800–893–5777.

English literary studies monograph series
ISSN 0829-7681 ; 88
Includes bibliographical references.
ISBN-10 0-920604-83-8
ISBN-13 is 978-0-920604-83-0

CONTENTS

Introduction

The Poet of Ear and Eye

One might wish that the earlier criticism of Robert Frost had been richer, more oriented to close reading and less diverted by the dismaying results of biographical research. (And yet are they not always dismaying?) Indeed, the prospective writer is faced with an odd situation: one confronts a poet of obvious distinction and complexity yet feels a vague sense of critical neglect. Perhaps it is not neglect exactly, but one is aware of large and curious gaps. The contrast with other figures in American poetry is striking. One need only think of the volume of work devoted to Pound, Williams, and Stevens to feel a discrepancy. And yet who is this writer about whom so much and so little has been written? The very name has an aura about it — Frost: to speak it aloud in certain circles is almost inevitably to invite condescension.

Nothing is more pointless than literary polemics, and I shall not attempt to make a case for Frost's post-modernity, nor to apply to his work any method derived exclusively from a particular critical school or theorist. I would like, however, to attempt to see him in a context that is somewhat different from the one he is often associated with. In doing so, I would like to claim for him a continuing relevance to contemporary readers that transcends that of any critical orthodoxy. And yet I intend no major heresy. We have learned from various critics to see his work against a background of Jamesian pragmatism as this in turn is viewed against the cultural context created by the legacies of Emerson and of Thoreau. Richard Poirier has completed this picture by demonstrating how Frost utilized an array of British poetic models for his own ends. I consider myself the beneficiary of this previous work and hope to build upon it in various ways. Yet I hope to keep always in view the need for close reading of the texts and for a careful attunement to their aesthetic qualities. This I think is something that, oddly, has not always been sufficiently attended to in criticism of this poet who, of all American writers, achieved perhaps the most refined and subtle effects of style. My general approach, therefore, will be to examine representative poems and to read them in a way that will be as attentive as possible to their subtleties of diction, metaphor, rhythm, and tone. Beyond this, I would like to use these readings as markers to chart a path through the

Collected Poems as a whole. Heidegger speaks of a poet having but one thought to which all his work is dedicated, a ground note out of which it arises and to which it gives some form of expression in each individual poem. Is it possible to locate such a thought for this writer? Could this be what previous scholarship has missed in being diverted by peripheral concerns?

The Path Across the Field

The beginning of my thesis may be suggested by a metaphor of direction. It seems to me that Frost's poetry taken as a whole exhibits a certain movement outward, away from its initial late-Romantic self-involvement (or what I will characterize as such) and toward an outlook which embraces realities external to that self, external in fact to any self or selves, and eventually external to the human as such. The result at first is an accommodation of those aspects of reality that are unpredictable, resistant, or dangerous. In fact, it requires that the poet affirm the fact of death, or mortal limitation generally. It also forces on him an increased awareness of the smallness and apparent insignificance of human effort and the limitation of knowledge. There is an increased and more detailed awareness of the natural world, and, eventually, a sense that the needs of the environment and those of human beings might be in conflict. These realizations tend to be expressed in dramatic terms — as encounters between actors, as enactments of a dramatically situated speaker, and as modulations of a speaking voice in a context. His imagination seems essentially dramatic in this limited sense. Though the encounter is sometimes between a human subject and the natural world, there is yet even at those times scene, tension, dramatic focus, voice — and, with these, some element of risk. There is a repeated placing of the human subject in a situation of exposure. This dramatizing inclination is a further means by which the late-Romantic starting point of the work as a whole is challenged and changed, and along with it its implicit anthropocentrism.

Thus though there is this expressive focus in a speaking voice and on persons and personal relations in the narratives, the work moves beyond these concerns, and indeed beyond the concerns of human beings narrowly considered. We might even say that, on the one hand, the *Collected Poems* seems like the account of the development of one particular poet and his beginnings in a lush and evocative lyricism; at the same time it seems to present the archetypal image of the maturation of any given individual. There seems also to be, though, a larger implication, a specifically historical one, having to do in fact with the fate of the West. The work is a profound meditation on selfhood but an even more profound meditation on the place of human beings in the world, and it creates a parable applicable both to individuals and to humans as a species. I might characterize this as one of awakening to consciousness amid the experience of beauty, and then of being prompted to move beyond this initial starting point, partly by one's own energies, partly by the demands of the world. In the process of this exploration — a trial that is the very pattern of education itself — we encounter not merely our flaws but our fragility and smallness, and, again, this is presented in such a way as to suggest both individual and collective meanings. An individual may come to see him or herself as insignificant, and likewise as a species we may at moments come to seem to ourselves insignificant against the background of the world as an ecological totality. One is brought to such feelings both by the tremendous presences of nature as well as by the bewildering processes of its inner life, both minute, and intricate. It is perhaps this latter perception in particular — that of the intricacy of organic life — which prompts a recognition, ultimately, of the fragility of nature itself.

And yet we cannot and we do not discover such fundamental realities other than through perception. Though there are times when Frost's skeptical metaphoric play becomes itself a major concern in the poetry, creating a poetry about the process of comprehension, a poetry of inquiry, of ambiguity, of epistemological questioning, and sometimes of perplexity, it is not merely metaphor which interests him, not merely the "play" of metaphors, but the way it can be used to explore the world which is definitely "there," and unquestionably a real and pressing concern. Even at his most skeptical, he nevertheless demands of his figures that they evoke some sense of the real, as difficult as it might be to say definitively what that reality is, or how it should be described. Frost's writing in fact is continually solicited by the complexity and interrogative nature of perception itself and constitutes an extended and nuanced demonstration of the perceptual life and its discovery and exploration of the world. For this reason the concepts we find in phenomenology, and in particular in Merleau-Ponty, on the nature of perception and its broader ontological implications are particularly relevant for understanding this body of poetry.

> We must understand that this red under my eyes is not, as is always said, a quale, a pellicle of being without thickness, a message at the same time indecipherable and evident, which one has or has not received, but of which, if one has received it, one knows all there is to know, and of which in the end there is nothing to say. It requires a focusing, however brief; it emerges from a less precise, more general redness, in which my gaze was caught, into which it sank, before – as we put it so aptly – fixing it. And, now that I have fixed it, if my eyes penetrate into it, into its fixed structure, or if they start to

wander round about again, the quale resumes its atmospheric existence. Its precise form is bound up with a certain wooly, metallic, or porous configuration or texture, and the quale itself counts for very little compared with these participations. (*The Visible and the Invisible* 131)

For Merleau-Ponty perception occurs in an interrogative engagement with objects. We do not merely register perceptions in a single and total grasp; we explore them, question them, accept them into ourselves and allow our sensibility to be directed by them. Perception is in a sense always and continually unfolding; it is an open process always unfinished and always revealing still more. It is never a plenum, never a completely fulfilled and self-present whatness; it is rather a continual beckoning and a lure. The reason for this does not have to do merely with the constitution of our faculties: the perceptions we have are not truncated versions of some more complete or more accurate ones we would have if the limitations of our faculties were somehow overcome. Our perceptions have this interrogative and unfinished character because the world itself does also. It too is radically in process and consists — as we learn from the novel ontology developed at various points in Merleau-Ponty's writing — of levels, breaks, points of punctuation, and indeterminate declinations from equally fluctuating norms. It is never fixed but always tends toward a burgeoning. It is James's buzzing and blooming confusion, though indeed it is often not confused but exhibits order, periodicity, and always, and in abundance, shape, pattern, aesthetic form — often quite delicate and precise — and complex ranges of sensuous allure. Frost's style, though possessed of a powerful visual sense, a certain chasteness, and always a defining clarity, has also a characteristic delicacy and tact before the salient detail of the world. And yet it has equally a kind of wavering and unfixed quality, a way of hovering among possibilities, of venturing descriptions in tentative and suggestive ways while at the same time holding out the possibility of their immediate revision.

This characteristic has been remarked on more than once, and sometimes in pejorative terms. It is decried as spiritual drifting or condescended to as mere charm, or perhaps even confusion.[1] In reality, though, it enacts the process of perceptual discovery in its openness and lability. At the same time it discovers and discloses for us through this discovery, the nature of the physical world in its manifold process devoid of definite conclusions. Consider Alphonso Lingis's powerful restatement of this essentially process-oriented vision of reality:

The sensible itself exists, Maurice Merleau-Ponty says, in the interrogative mode. The sensible that we encounter when we look, listen, smell, and touch is not an answer to a questioning that is only in us, is not a plenum that fills in a blank opened by us, a positum that is the affirmative answer to our inquiries. The sensible is there as the surfacing of a depth, a crest on a wave that pursues its way. Our eyes touch lightly over the things, just enough to recognize on them the functions the program of our everyday concerns have put on them, but when we look beneath this human function to their sensible natures our eyes discover in the color, our ears in the resonance, not something that is just what it is here and now, without mystery, but something like a quest they join, a tone on its way calling forth echoes and responses — a red come from its own past, responding not to our question but to its own, seeking its redness beyond the moment and elsewhere, water seeking its liquidity in the sunlight rippling across the cypresses in the back of the garden. (*The Imperative* 29)

We can readily see how this is similar to passages we find in Thoreau, in Emerson, and in Whitman. Frost brings his own particular accent to it repeatedly in virtually all he writes and hence in a variety of modes and moods. Let us consider two particularly clear examples.

SPRING POOLS

These pools that, though in forests, still reflect
The total sky almost without defect,
And like the flowers beside them, chill and shiver,
Will like the flowers beside them soon be gone,
And yet not out by any brook or river,
But up by roots to bring dark foliage on.

The trees that have it in their pent-up buds
To darken nature and be summer woods —
Let them think twice before they use their powers
To blot out and drink up and sweep away
These flowery waters and these watery flowers
From snow that melted only yesterday.

In this poem we find a modern variant of the Romantic moment of epiphany: the world lies open to the inquiring gaze, and we momentarily glimpse the apparent wholeness of nature, which here seems composed of calm and abiding entities — a stilled earthly pool and a perfectly reflected heaven. Earth and sky comprise a harmony, existing in momentary poise. This in turn is apprehended by a perfectly comprehending consciousness, one that is preternaturally calm and passively apprehending the order of nature in an instant of unmediated perception. Yet almost at once a host of qualifying perceptions crowds into awareness: the reader must remain in a kind of suspense, in fact, for the sentence is not yet complete, and we cannot seize upon this image of stillness as upon a final truth. With the third line the image of the pools is altered: a barely perceptible activity is ascribed to them — they "chill and shiver." What had seemed a perfect stillness now betrays a subtle activity operating below the threshold created by our initial inspection, which now appears as a defining level, founded even as it is surpassed.

Moreover, the comparison with the brief spring flowers adds the idea of transitoriness. In this way, the original clarity is undermined by the subtle suggestions of change. The poet does not lament this. Instead he attempts to track its full extent in so far as possible, imagining the various transformations the pools must go through. There is thus a change in the nature of his awareness, which itself begins to move from one of meditative stasis to a searching and hypothetical projecting, in which he attempts to imagine the process by which the pools are absorbed by the roots of trees and by the trees themselves and their eventual buds, leaves, and flowers, a process which will "bring dark foliage on." Things in nature do not exist separately but interact, at times in barely perceptible ways. The very smoothness of the verse suggests the ease with which they are transformed one into another. The visual clarity of the outset has been displaced by an awareness of ambiguity and process, for the speaker has become aware that one cannot speak of solid entities so much as of graduated phases which in their manifold character lure sense perception outward into the world and yet lead it also beyond any single and given perception. It is as if the awareness of the flux and ambiguity of nature has darkened the clear mirror of the opening lines. For the most part the poet's attitude toward this is calm and accepting. In the concluding lines, however, he voices what seems to be a desire for at least a momentary respite from change:

> Let them think twice before they use their powers
> To blot out and drink up and sweep away
> These flowery waters and these watery flowers
> From snow that melted only yesterday.

The first line seems almost wistful with this desire and with the simultaneous recognition that it can never be satisfied. The poet changes his tone almost at once, though, and the second line with its massed verbs is strong with the suggestion of the power of change itself. The third line emphasizes one of the implications of this with its wonderful image of "flowery waters and watery flowers." Like Monet's water lily paintings, such a line creates an image of the ambiguous nature of reality: not only is nothing exactly what it is or what it seems, but its very phenomenal appearance is ambiguous and multi-dimensional, a thing to be explored and questioned, and whose aspects are never entirely in themselves simple and single, but rather multiple and manifold, never perfectly self-present but infused with a power of self-differentiation, self-dispersal, and self-undermining. It is as if nature questions itself even as we question it. It exists in a continuous transition from moment to moment, each merely an abstraction of convenience singled out by the inquiring gaze, a temporarily fixed level from which it departs to venture among an infinitely divisible and extensible continuum.

The poem concludes with an implicit recognition of mortality in a line reminiscent of the medevial "ubi sunt" or "où sont les neiges" motif. Despite this, and despite the epistemological ambiguities that have multiplied, the speaker remains poised and calm in the midst of these potentially confusing forces. Perhaps we might see the strange lines which begin "let them think twice . . . " as masking such an awareness of death: our inability to definitively interpret the physical world calls to mind the uncertainty of all human things, including our being itself, as well as the impersonal destructive force of natural process. Consciousness can penetrate into nature, but only up to a point. It can then extend this by means of imagination; yet, again, only so far. The limitations — but more precisely the complexity — of perception and knowledge are made apparent to the perceiving and speaking subject even in the very moment of perception and the very act of speaking, and with this comes a sense of the ecological situatedness of any individual, of one's striking imaginative and conceptual possibilities — to glimpse the orders of nature in their movement and process — but also of the limits of any one life taken in itself.

In "Hyla Brook," similar themes are presented but in such a way that the spectatorial character of the speaker, which was a prominent feature of "Spring Pools," is replaced with a subtle concept of joyous participation in the temporal change of the world as this is manifest in, and in a sense mediated by, the crucial, sometimes philosophically overlooked, fact of its seasonal order.

HYLA BROOK

By June our brook's run out of song and speed.
Sought for much after that, it will be found
Either to have gone groping underground
(And taken with it all the Hyla breed
That shouted in the mist a month ago,
Like ghost of sleigh bells in a ghost of snow) —

Or flourished and come up in jewelweed,
Weak foliage that is blown upon and bent,
Even against the way its waters went.
Its bed is left a faded paper sheet
Of dead leaves stuck together by the heat —
A brook to none but who remember long.
This as it will be seen is other far
Than with brooks taken otherwhere in song.
We love the things we love for what they are.

The paradox of this poem is that we are never presented with the brook itself, as we might expect to be. Instead, we are given a virtual inventory of the transformations that it goes through at different times of the year: it is a small trickle in June (when it has "run out of song and speed") or is completely dry shortly after; there is also a brief glance backward to the spring with its mists and croaking frogs. This is in contrast to the typical Romantic landscape or river sonnet such as practiced by Coleridge and Wordsworth. In this genre we are usually given a picture of the natural scene as we would expect it to be: if it is a river, its torrent or placid flow are evoked; if London Bridge at dawn, we see the town and its roofs in the early light, bright and glittering in the smokeless air. From there we move to some generalization that emerges out of the natural description. In this poem, Frost seems to deliberately avoid this practice, creating a perspectival presentation of the world by means of the fact of seasonal change. In a sense the poem enacts a fundamental phenomenological principle, that of the perspectival character of knowledge and its temporal formation.

Thus, to begin with, the heat and dryness of the brook bed in summer are wonderfully evoked. Yet the rapid barrage of images seems intended to convey a sense of continuous transformation rather than to describe a definite entity. It is as if it is necessary to engage in this rapid play of metaphors — not for its own sake, but in order to evoke the reality of the object and by extension of the world. At the same time the appearance of the dry brook is vividly rendered: it is "a faded paper sheet / Of dead leaves stuck together by the heat." This is a starting point for an enlarged conception which moves by a process of continuous metaphorical substitution, turning the cube of reality, each image bringing some aspect of the actual into focus then picking up another, then another, in a potentially endless series of illuminations by which the metaphorical reveals momentarily the nature of the world, not in a definitive way, but in an uncertain, yet vital temporal engagement which is the mind's participation in the continuous chain of transformations of reality itself. Hence the last line: for though we do not know what the brook is, we yet are acquainted with it. We might say we have lived alongside it, and that its varied activity has become part of our own, an element in our imaginative life as well as our physical life. Our connection to it is a participation in the being of something outside ourselves. Yet the continuous transformation of metaphor which is the result of this attention is a necessary part of that very participation, both as cause and as result. In our endless attention, the appearance of the loved object is continually changing, as is our understanding of it. Thus, the deepest connection one can have with the world is this paying attention, an attention which does not "observe" but participates in its reality. In this sense, this "play of surfaces" is itself depth, and hence it justifies the use of the charged word *love* and indicates that this play is not mere play, and that the surfaces in question are absolutely real, despite their transitory and perspectival nature.

This movement outward into the realm of the contingent, the temporal, and the uncertain is itself enacted in the style of the work as well as in its content. The author attempts to create a style at once realistically transparent in registering the minutia of the physical and social worlds yet also sophisticated about its fictionality. He has no illusions about the ease of "mirroring" the external world, yet he does continually look to such an external environment as the ultimate test of the validity of metaphor and of thought in general. Yet for all that, we know also that the world remains enigmatic. The understanding has various tools, yet at best they move only a certain way into the darkness, and their purchase on reality is always a matter of conjecture and, in a sense, of solicitude — a solicitude for the understanding itself and also for the world, a solicitude which requires of these images, these metaphors, these concepts a continual and responsive circumspection and adjustment.

Thus the recent discussions of Merleau-Ponty are timely with respect to the discussion of Frost's work, for they make us aware once again of the primacy of perception and of literary representations of it. After an extended period in which attention was focused on other matters — the diacritical organization of language and other sign systems, for example — literary criticism must now return to questions of perception and the exploration of the perceptual life through language and descriptions. Such a turn, such a return, is implied and required by the recent concerns with embodiment — in its various manifestations — and with environmental questions, which must remain abstract and uncompelling in the absence of direct depictions of the realities in question. Yet in addition to what we have already seen in the passages from Merleau-Ponty and Alphonso Lingis, what does perception reveal — if anything — that is of special significance to this particular poet, something perhaps not so markedly or so powerfully captured by any other?

The Limits and the Boundaries of Things

It is perhaps the specific awareness of liminality, of bordering, that is particularly important for Frost's work. He always seems especially aware of how phenomena shade into each other, of how they are not describable as entities whose characteristics can be determinately fixed in positive descriptions but must rather be tentatively characterized, explored with a descriptive intention in which surmise and hypothesis dominate over assertion. We find fluid shifts in metaphor, metaphor modified in its emphasis by a questioning or even facetious tone, and other means — sometimes of a subtleness that challenges critical characterization — by which a fixed and iconic conception of the poem is questioned and dispersed. The poet wonders aloud and invites us to do so with him; he seems half-amused at his own images and proposes others, allows our attention to drift away from the scene he has presented and to consider variations on it, moving his descriptive presentation fluidly in hypothetical alternatives through time, space, and circumstance. We have seen instances of some of this in the two short pieces just looked at: the brook is imagined at other times and in other seasons, the path of the water from the pools (which are themselves melted snow) is imagined moving through the roots of trees and up into leaves, tracked through a process of imaginative hypothesis. Yet it is not merely flux and process which are the subject of his descriptions, nor mere ambiguity as such; it is rather the indeterminateness of the boundaries in nature itself between one state, one condition, one thing, and those which are conjoined with it in space or in time. We notice a similar focus at times in A.R. Ammons, and, in the art of painting, Milton Avery is known for paying great attention to just this aspect of reality. It is given analytical attention in Merleau-Ponty's concept of the level, to which we have already alluded, and which Alphonso Lingis, his most able American expositor (and translator), has made the subject of some of his own finest passages of phenomenological description.

We might ask ourselves how often Frost's work avoids determinate, definite, and fixed characterizations in favor of suggestive presentations which ask the reader's imagination to move questioningly among a range of possibilities, and to take in with them the subtle borderings, the fine shadings, which are so crucial in our understanding of the specific realities of the world, and for grasping them accurately in their nature. In this peculiar and special emphasis, his work differs from the concretist and objectivist work of such writers as Williams, Pound, and Moore whose writing is often focused on discrete objects and discrete states of affairs (hence the apt term Objectivism). And yet to place such ambiguity and such borderings in the foreground of one's imagination is also, by implication, to foreground the very fact of the primordial *fragility* of the things of the world. For it is at their borders that things are most vulnerable, exposed to the contingencies of the environment, to the impingements of other things, to the ontological fact of exposure itself, the being held out into the nothing, as Heidegger might phrase it.

Economy

In *The Accursed Share*, *Erotism*, and other works Georges Bataille constructs a vision of nature in which it is seen as continually exceeding itself in an on-going surplus. This constant surplus production of energy, of life, of species, and of individuals is based, in Bataille's view, on the essentially unlimited surplus of energy originating in the sun. This continual over-profusion Bataille refers to as "general economy." It is an essentially Nietzschean concept of the continual and non-teleological self-exceeding of nature as a whole. Yet Bataille also proposes a second concept, what he calls "restricted economies." These are the individual creatures that do not possess an infinite store of energy but only a limited one and so must organize and safeguard their own existence. There is, therefore, a dual order: that of limited and highly organized beings who must limit their expenditures of energy and safeguard themselves, and then, as a source and background, an unlimited profusion characterized by surplus and excess. Certainly there are no direct connections between Bataille and Frost. The very mention of their names together in the same sentence seems anomalous. Yet we find continually in the latter's poetry the expression of ideas of exactly this kind, and an encompassing vision of the natural world that is remarkably similar. Perhaps the similarity is to be explained by reference to a common source in post-Darwinian and post-Nietzschean intellectual history. However that may be, there can be no doubt that the parallels are striking and all the more so given the total dissimilarity of their respective *oeuvres* in every other way. It sometimes seems as though two entirely dissimilar writers had nonetheless, in certain respects, exactly the same thoughts.

One has only to consider the number of times Frost gives expression to the need for limit and definition, as though without these there would be a danger of engulfment of some kind, perhaps in the boundless *apeiron* of Plato and Levinas. Indeed this aspect of his personality is well known: good fences make good neighbors, we are told in an implicit expression of the need for limit and demarcation. He gives these words to a character, it is true, and one we are to understand as rather dull and unimaginative. Yet it is not so much that the narrator questions this need for limits, but rather only his neighbor/interlocutor's way of thinking about them. Again in "Triple Bronze" and "A Drumlin Woodchuck" we find similar ideas. And yet there is a deeper level, certainly. These last two pieces are hardly among Frost's best poems. It seems rather to be the case that in these slighter works he makes explicit what is more deeply implied in much of the rest of his writing: a deeper sense of limit, a deeper sense of how limit, finitude, boundary, and demarcation characterize existence and in particular organic existence at the most fundamental level.

Yet perhaps to understand this thought we must entertain what amounts to an opposite one. Do we not find also in his work expressions of profusion? Of an exceeding of all limits in unbounded surplus — ideas we could associate with Bataille's "general economy"? It is perhaps a less often seen aspect, and something not as readily associated with his name. Yet in "After Apple-Picking" we see the intuitive perception of a depthless and boundless fecundity associated with the night itself beneath the individual images that appear before the speaker's eye (or "I"), which is itself a further depth, that of his individual existence — the rapt enthrallment of his individual dream, which is also his own life; in "To Earthward" we see the presentation of an excess of emotion, of affect, welling up within the individual and used as the means to approach an unmediated contact with the reality of the world itself in its *thisness*, and then in fact with death, a surplus resident within the individual and impelling him or her toward an ecstatic and even self-rending encounter with otherness; and, finally, in the late poem "The Pod of Milkweed" we are told quite specifically that "waste was of the essence of the scheme," the scheme being the totality of nature as it moves through its continual evolution. Yet to perceive both facts — the essential boundedness of any organic existence *and* the boundless profusion that moves beneath it and is its background and source — is also and finally to perceive the deeper sense of limit I mentioned earlier. For every existent is bounded not only by its inherent limits but exists in a context of waste and expendability. It is unique and yet almost instantly replaced nonetheless; it is perfect and integral in its structure and design, which bring it into relief against the formless process it arises out of, and yet it is continually eaten away by this very process which moves ceaselessly within it and dissolves it in the flux of temporality, resolving its individuality back into the order of Being in general.

Yet in Frost this vision is given a peculiar inflection and perhaps a peculiar pathos. For the very terms in which he thinks, the very materials, the images, the metaphors with which his imagination operates are drawn so completely from the organic world, as well as from the human world of villages and farms whose inhabitants he regards with a naturalism that perhaps makes of them yet more natural creatures, yet more perishing and transient natural forms, without, however, lessening their special humanity — in fact quite the contrary — that his work is almost inevitably permeated by a sense of the delicacy of every natural creature, the fragility of every natural form, a delicacy and a fragility which his style in its clarity, precision, and nuance attempts to convey, to do a discreet and aesthetic justice to, to depict in limpid and beautiful language in which the forms of nature and those of culture seem to become one and to express the transient beauty and boundless fragility of the world itself.

The Plight of the World

What we might call the plight of the world consists in this very fragility, combined, quite simply, with the fact of our very presence in it, the presence of humans. For it is our capacity to create abstractions in part based upon metaphors and images which allow us to manipulate the world, to shape our life according to our own desires and to pull ourselves partly out of the matrix of nature from which we arise, which also gives us the capacity to damage this matrix itself. We act in the world and shape our lives according to the metaphors we create. Yet our actions have unsuspected consequences upon this very world, whose complexity we cannot always grasp. It seems to me that Frost was one of the first modern writers to fully appreciate this complex, perhaps unameliorable situation. Is it possible for humans to exist in the world, pursuing their human desires, as in fact they must, without destroying it?

And yet a philosophy which enables us to appreciate the manifold and complex processes of nature in their particularity, nuance, and inherent dynamism gives us some means of perhaps fashioning a way of thought, a way of life less invasive, less destructive to the world and to ourselves. Is it possible that it could illuminate the human and nonhuman both, that along with fostering a greater respect and circumspection with regard to nature, it could also foster a greater awareness of our own potentials — our potential for renewal, for creativity, for an openness to ourselves and to the world? Merleau-Ponty provides us with a philosophy of nuance and non-dualistic wholism. Yet in the thought of Deleuze we find a further element we need in our two-fold task of fashioning a conceptual scheme adequate to Frost's poetry, and then, beyond that, to the reality of our situation in the contemporary world — in which we are only too powerful to damage it and only too powerless to reform our life both individually and collectively, only too capable, given the technology we enjoy, and yet strangely unable to renew the creative force of numerous aspects of our culture.

In the work of Gilles Deleuze we find a contemporary philosophy which constructs itself as a vision of creative process — the creative process embodied in the natural world, as well as the creative in its specifically human manifestations. That is to say, the philosophy is a process philosophy in the manner of Whitehead, James, and Bergson, yet we find in it also a type of vitalism appropriate to a post-modern era which has absorbed the results of modern physics and biology, and especially the latter, and which, in addition, finds itself in a type of cultural crisis.[2] And yet if it does have these general features, it is in a non-dogmatic fashion and puts itself forward more in the form of thought experiments than in the form of fixed doctrine. It is interesting that some of the major influences on Deleuze's thought are exactly those thinkers Frost himself was drawn to, in large part because of their orientation toward nature, as well as natural science, and their general feeling for the process of experience and the encompassing processes of the world in which it finds itself.

Deleuze perhaps goes further than these in displacing human beings from the center of his picture of reality. Yet here also he is strangely prefigured by aspects of Frost's work, since the latter, especially in his late poetry, tends to question the centrality of humans to the world and, if he remains always at last within the realm of humanism very broadly considered, seems to push against it and toward a broader ecological vision. Yet Delueze's post-humanist orientation is not attended by any sort of pessimism with respect to human existence. In fact, he tends to be at pains to project a vision of possibilities and of the experimentation necessary to realize them, without, for all that, falling into some sort of naïve optimism. He distances himself from fashionable forms of pessimism sometimes associated with the post-modern and in particular with that form of cultural pessimism that is always proclaiming the death of this or that — whether it be metaphysics or philosophy altogether. It is striking to consider that Frost might actually be more pessimistic than Deleuze when one considers the sheer range of human suffering his work takes detailed account of and when one further considers the still more important suggestion, increasingly evident in his later work, of a fundamental incompatibility between modern western culture and nature itself. Yet the refusal of easy and fashionable forms of pessimism nonetheless creates a strong resonance between this body of work and the type of philosophy Deleuze attempts to create, and Frost's concern with traditional forms of beauty in literature is a tendency which is somewhat analogous to Deleuze's interest in traditional forms of system building in philosophy. This last is not a parallel I wish to emphasize, and it plays little role in what follows, but it points out in both authors a way that they have of distancing themselves from some of the more obvious tendencies in modern culture, at least as these affected their respective disciplines, in an effort to reach toward deeper levels of analysis in which the true problems — and potentials — of human existence could be more fully grasped. The fundamental problem I see both addressing is the basic question of how to find value in human existence in a post-anthropocentric context, a problem that is deeper than that of "the end of metaphysics" or, say, "breaking the pentameter."

Difference and Repetition/Belief in the World

> *Difference and Repetition* is decidedly modern in the way in which it places a notion of variation at the center of its unfolding and enfolding of a thinking of difference and repetition. Variation, Deleuze notes in his 1994 preface, is not added to either difference or repetition in order to conceal their true nature (an originary being of identity through self-sameness and self-presence). Rather, it is the case that variation is repetition's constitutive element, it is its interiority which guarantees that what is repeated is not merely a return of the same but the differentiation of difference as a productive and positive power. (Pearson 81)

More specifically, Deleuze's concern with the theme of repetition turns out to be surprisingly relevant to some of the deeper patterns of thought we find in Frost. His tendency to seek tentative illumination, the momentary stay against confusion which we have looked at from the standpoint of Merleau-Ponty's "being in the interrogative mode," has also the implication that this experience, this event, will be re-visited, or in fact that this moment itself is such a revisiting. There is, therefore, implied in this poetics of suggestiveness and indeterminacy a concern with repetition and with the way this specific fact — the return of situations, of moments, of tasks in the course of day-to-day life (and Frost's poetry is very much the poetry of day-to-day) — acts upon humans. Is it a power of entropic degeneration, finally? Is human experience merely a sort of wearing down? Can there be ways of finding more in it than what might seem to be present at first glance? Our discussion here is necessarily schematic and simplified, yet these are exactly some of the themes that Deleuze deals with in *Difference and Repetition,* despite the abstractness of its idiom (though it is not always so). Any reader of Frost will recognize them instantly as some of his ongoing concerns. Moreover, if we do imagine that there is more to the repetition in our lives than meets the eye at first, are we deluded? How is it possible to evaluate where insight leaves off and mere fantasy begins? And how, finally, is it possible to embody in action and habit some of the powers of enlargement and creativity we sometimes glimpse in ourselves and in nature?

Here the practical and concrete orientation of Frost's work becomes particularly significant, for the repetition that especially preoccupies him is one associated with labor. We might even see a certain class aspect here as well, one which is decidedly working-class in its orientation, despite the author's occasional conservative pronouncements, for it is laborers, housewives, migrant farm workers and ordinary farmers and laboring persons of small rural towns who endure the power of repetition in its harshest form and with the least to mediate its effects, effects of fatigue, aging, and illness mental and physical. Yet aside from such potentially political considerations, in its content and style, the poetry often seems like an embodiment of the central question of whether life can be imagined as other than entropic decay, placing the question against a background of a post-humanist conception of nature.

Belief in the World

Does the world, then, hold out for us, the humans, only problems or are there potentials as well? Strictly speaking, we cannot say in advance. Yet even if our control of nature could be extended to some ultimately conceivable limit, we must always be subject to time itself, and to chance and mortality. Human existence contains and implies always a suffering, an anguish, based upon our creaturely existence. Indeed in Frost's poetry, it is marked by brutalizing physical labor, by early death, poverty, and by hardships of all kinds. Some of this is imposed by social factors, and yet some would seem to be inherent in the human situation as such — the peculiar vulnerability of delicate and peculiarly unstable creatures who yet have the capacity to extricate themselves part way from their biological context, to transcend it in the ambiguous adventure of culture, and yet never to transcend it entirely. This situation perhaps gives rise to a special pessimism. Is human existence worth it? It may be that the poet — at first and for a long time inspired by the beauty of the natural world, which he records in his language and images — undergoes a gradual darkening of vision, so that at length he is inclined to answer in the negative. We will make no attempt to develop this as a thesis. Indeed, it could be merely a trick of light — a dark light refracted, as it were, from the polished surfaces of the work and onto the personal sensibility of one particular critic. Yet regardless of what we might feel the author's attitude actually was, it is more significant that his work, taken as a whole, does seem to give rise to the question. Is there an ongoing redemptive power in beauty itself, however, and specifically the beauty of nature? Deleuze speaks of his late film project as an effort to elucidate the conditions for what he called belief in the world, a belief he felt was in danger in post-war or contemporary culture, and whose restoration he found one basis for in modern cinema. His concern there is not with nature, but it is to a significant extent with seeing, with light and visibility itself. Where these are, there is beauty. When Frost sees, he sees the beauty of nature. Could this awareness of beauty, penetrating deeply enough into one's awareness, become the factor that would cause one to feel that the task of human existence was worth it after all? Particularly when it is combined with a post-anthropocentric perspective in which humans (and their desires) are not necessarily the most important things in the world? Could the awareness of beauty be analogous to the awareness of God which Deleuze explicates in Spinoza — a beatitude that is always available and which yet promises and confers nothing, or which promises nothing and yet confers the world as it is?[3]

Part One: The Poetry of Embowerment and the Poetry of Education

Introduction to Part One

In Part One our purpose is to look at how Frost's mature style emerges from its late-Romantic beginnings. We locate these beginnings, specifically, in the Pre-Raphaelite style as it is seen in Rossetti, and we observe there in particular one of its most important characteristics — its tendency to deal with all experience as a type of reverie. We attempt to determine this style's underlying purpose through a kind of phenomenological analysis. Its purpose, it seems clear, is to insulate the self that speaks in the poems from the disruptive or unforeseeable aspects of experience through the creation of an artificial consistency of temporal flow and an artificially devised self-presence of sense impressions. It is language itself, of course, which is the medium for the creation of this alternative version of natural experience in which the contingent is made less pressing, the uncertain less hazardous, and in which what is gratifying — agreeable sensation — is made in some sense more so by being prolonged through an array of elaborate stylistic effects. Style, therefore draws our attention very strongly in this work, yet always with an eye toward determining its underlying intention. We then attempt to trace these tendencies in Frost's early poetry. Yet at almost the same time we are forced to observe in it the beginnings of subtle departures from this Pre-Raphaelite orientation and thus also from the underlying motives which that approach served. However, Frost is in some respects a cautious and circumspect writer. He does not progress by means of breaks and repudiations of his early manner but by narrow modifications of it, gently leading it in a different direction. For this reason we attempt to trace the incremental passage by which he moves away from certainty, enclosue, and plenitude and toward alterity, toward the contingent, the open, and the resistant. At the end of Chapter One, we look at one of his mature pieces, "The Silken Tent," and attempt to see how, though very close to the early style in many ways, it nonetheless makes greater room for what cannot be assimilated into the subject's own reverie, in this case the Beloved in her otherness.

Chapter Two charts the further excursions of the poet into areas of experience which are marked by alterity in their basic nature and which cannot be brought within the confines of his early mode but demand something else. The most basic form of alterity is time and, related to that, repetition.[1] A reading of the poem "Birches" shows it to be in part about the problem of making repetition into a positive power of ongoing renewal. As such it points out how far the author has already come from the world of his early work. Here he needs, and finds, a poetic which can encounter growth and change. Yet in so doing it must also encounter the great power which brings about the opposite of growth — mere repetition which has the ability to wear down, to bring about entropic degeneration. We see that here, in what might seem to be a rather naïve poem, the fundamental problem Deleuze deals with in *Difference and Repetition* is also dealt with — is it possible to think of life other than as a system that must inevitably run down? If so, how, and to what extent? Certainly it would not be possible to exhaust this theme with one poem, and in fact it is an on-going preoccupation of Frost's work. Here, though, we must be content with merely noting its presence and its importance, and observe just one of his treatments of it. It is a crucial treatment, however; for one thing, it foregrounds desire itself as a fundamental power in human existence. If it is possible to convert mere repetition into something creative and positive, this can be done only if the power of desire is given its full due in the overall economy of a life. The poem, therefore, takes the form of a kind of dialectic, a balancing of the buoyant power of desire and dream against the resistance of time and mortal fatigue.

And yet it may be that the greatest challenges to the author's imagination, as likewise to individuals in their attempt to live productively and creatively, comes not from time and aging but rather from the unforeseeable chances, the contingent and unpredictable, from that which is accidental and from the ways this tends to disrupt plans and to frustrate the pursuit of objectives. In fact we encounter this most often, or most tellingly, in our efforts to work productively. In the overall endeavor of work we are always encountering resistance — of others, of materials certainly, and the limitations imposed by time and circumstance — and contingency as the background of this resistance. These then are further forms of alterity which the poetry explores, and the topic of work becomes a natural means of doing so.

Fortunately we do not have to do things all by ourselves; every field of endeavor is also a social field, and even if the immediate context of our labor is solitary, we are by definition involved with others in the very fact of working. The social field has already organized the field of labor, for better or for worse. The clearest way of seeing the fundamental sociality of labor, however, is to consider what it is based upon. Working is always preceded by teaching. It is appropriate, therefore, that as we move further into the realm of the contingent and of work itself we find ourselves also encountering the fact of the interpersonal nature of labor as well as the process of teaching and initiation. These then become major themes in the middle parts of Chapter Two.

These first two chapters, therefore, mark out the entire range of styles the author explored, from the earliest to the fully mature. We track the change in his work which these styles indicate, and we attempt to see why such changes were needed. We note the shifting or qualified metaphors, the delicate stylistic touches which give evidence of his attentiveness to things, and likewise his attunement to the voices of the social world, and we note, finally, a greater factuality of language which yet does not give up its crucial investment in beauty and elegance.

Yet such stylistic characteristics and an attunement toward these forms of mere alterity cannot in themselves create a sufficiently complete image of experience. The violence inherent at some level in human experience must be dealt with too, both as it is manifest in forms of social exploitation and exclusion, and as it is seen in the violent impulses which seem to lurk in humans themselves and whose occasional irruption marks our social landscape with increasing frequency. These then are the last thematic points dealt with in Part One: they constitute a kind of pole opposite our starting point. Yet they show the furthest reach of the author's effort to stretch his technique, idiom, and manner to accommodate the demands of the real.

CHAPTER ONE

Embowered Expression

Frost's earliest poetry is written in a late-Romantic style that betrays the influence of Keats and the Pre-Raphaelites in its sensuousness, naturalism and pictorial character. Though comparisons between his poetry and Pre-Raphaelite poetry, especially that of Dante Gabriel Rossetti, have been made before, I would like to revisit this subject and spend some time describing this earliest phase of his style, particularly since I will later examine the ways in which he came to write differently.[1] And yet, as we shall see, he never really abandoned these earlier practices but incorporated them into a broader perspective and more flexible approach.

Sense Perception and the Libidinal Economy of Language

I have in mind a certain type of sensuous response, often accurate in detail, yet subtly inflected by an atmosphere of reverie. Reverie is perhaps a vague term, though it is one we find repeatedly associated with certain writers, such as Rousseau and Pater. Certainly the strangeness of Rossetti's poems has often been remarked, and with their dense texture and habit of mingling naturalistic detail with fantasy and elements of allegory, his sonnets and lyrics create a mannerist style whose effects are as curious as they are striking. Harold Bloom observes that when we read Rossetti's poems, we can never be sure if we are in the natural world or in some symbolic realm.[2] The two worlds, that of dream and of existence, seem to blend in poems like "The Woodspurge," "Autumn Idleness" or "Barren Spring." We might feel that in these short pieces he attempts to represent experience in a heightened and stylized way without in any sense leaving behind the natural world and its space, its visibility, and its light. Critics have spoken of the frozen quality of the depictions of nature that we find in Pre-Raphaelite painting, and this despite the minutely rendered natural detail. We see something similar in the poetry. And we might think of the work as showing two contradictory impulses: one toward a receptiveness of salient detail and another toward an occlusion of anything that would disrupt contemplation as such. A certain stillness is sought which yet is filled with sense perception and becomes, through that fullness and stillness, a kind of plenum of perception. In such painting, sense perception moves in every direction at once as a kind of hyper-alert potential, yet this very comprehensiveness is itself a type of immobility.

If the medium is language, things must be rather different. For language is not present in a simultaneity, as visual art can be; rather it is present temporally. Bergson and Deleuze have envisaged duration as wave-like continuities of various periodic lengths, overlapping and interacting in a complex persistence and fading. Reverie as a genre attempts to create the simultaneous presence of the pictorial by means of such durational events — as these are expressed in language and its conventions and genres. Such linguistic expression moves through time in a special way: consciousness is focused on an object or a scene, and a virtual cinema unfolds in recurrent phases of rhythm which overlap each other, lengthening out in sum their individually limited reaches, supplementing each other in a kind of leading on of perception. Perhaps such passages (they are seldom more) may be understood as the imagination's response to the foreignness of nature itself and to some ultimate dissatisfaction with natural experience, since there is a continual attempt to supplement perception, to enable it to achieve, in the medium of words, a more durable presence and self-presence than it naturally has. In this sense reverie attempts to alter the character of experience in order to make it more responsive to a desire for stasis and singularity and for singular satisfaction. In doing so, it must not only extend the natural fading away of phenomenal self-presence, but also exclude any disruptive elements in experience in favor of those which can be assimilated to its fundamental purpose of creating seamless trances in which anything resembling Benjamin's shock experience is entirely excluded, for, after all, shocks of that kind are not only characteristic of urban modernity: we might think of them as part of natural experience as such and as being most often seen in the basic experience of surprise. Reverie, by contrast, seeks to establish states in which consciousness is both heightened and yet allowed to remain in some sense undisturbed, and in which a kind of self-consistency of temporal experience, an evenness of flow in the experienced passage of time, is approached, albeit through the mediating substance of language itself. Though natural forms are acknowledged on the level of imagery, awareness is directed not toward those objects so much as back upon itself and upon its own (apparent) self-presence.[3]

In this context — the self-representation of an apparent self-presence — the linguistic medium itself cannot be ignored. Indeed the oddness of the descriptions, their very contrivance, reminds us that language is the enabling medium for these states we are attempting to characterize. They can indeed have no existence outside it. Literary language is therefore both a carrying medium (though not a transparent one) and an object of presentation. It directs attention to the object, which is often grasped in startling detail, yet it inflects the underlying self-perception of the subject, even at the level of sense perception, as well as at the level of temporal awareness. The poetry never leaves natural detail behind, nor does it leave behind the phenomenological givens of consciousness, nature, and the body. Yet it presents them through a dense and self-consciously contrived medium. Reverie is perhaps that genre which in fact makes it impossible to abandon phenomenological criticism while yet requiring, within that very context, a heightened awareness of the semiotic medium as well.

Portent and Exclusion: "The Woodspurge"

THE WOODSPURGE

The wind flapped loose, the wind was still,
Shaken out dead from tree and hill:
I had walked on at the wind's will, —
I sat now for the wind was still.

Between my knees my forehead was, —
My lips drawn in said not Alas!
My hair was over in the grass,
My naked ears heard the day pass.

My eyes, wide open, had the run
Of some ten weeds to fix upon;
Among that number, out of the sun,
The woodspurge flowered, three cups in one.

From perfect grief there need not be
Wisdom or even memory:
One thing then learnt remained to me, —
The woodspurge has a cup of three.

Rossetti's "The Woodspurge" begins by registering a natural fact. Yet one could hardly call the writing description, since it seems so deliberately inept if taken at that level; it is surprising, in fact, that the poem works at all, and yet it does. How strange, though, that the wind "flapped loose" and was "Shaken out dead from tree and hill." Direct experience, even of a surprising kind, as this would seem to be, is portrayed as being always already inflected by imaginative patterns, in this case the feeling that nature is in some peculiar way inert. Perhaps direct experience is even in some ways influenced by the resonances and echoings of words and phrases. Is our experience always partly "written" even before it is "direct," or perhaps in the very moment of its immediate apprehension? Consider Lyotard's observations, quoted with approval by Deleuze and Guattari in *Anti-Oedipus*:

> Words are not signs, but by means of words the thing becomes visible and yet is seen to have other aspects, facets which we do not immediately see, to be revealed later, to another gaze, or perhaps never. Things become themselves signs by this means, yet in the sense that we see the word in them, which thus in this way comes to be visible in itself. (*Anti-Oedipus* 204)

Yet it would be wrong to say that there is no direct experience; the poem shows us that sense perception presses upon us and is always, and repeatedly, *surprising*. The wind does sometimes seem a thing that flaps loose, the details of the world do sometimes loom up in perception with a strange intensity, with an auratic salience and clarity, so that they seem to be signs and portents, as they do in this poem (though portents of what, we do not know). Yet it would be equally wrong to say that there is a pure and unmediated access to the world. There is always a kind of fusion; there is both dream and existence, both the *word* that echoes (and the imaginative patterns absorbed from reading or from viewing art), and then there is the naked ear, the naked eye, which takes in the *world* as it passes in its phenomenal, mute, and enigmatic givenness. In this type of writing, the steady and fluid rhythm, the metrical prolonging of this fusion of dream and perception, is in fact prolonged in such a way that we are able to recognize both elements clearly, and likewise their coexistence and their interpenetration.

Yet still, as we have already partly observed, the description is nonetheless effective at a certain reportorial level; it has its own peculiar accuracy and suggests a natural context which, though in some ways apparently lifeless, yet retains a power to provoke intense sensation. One exists in a continual state of exposure to the world, despite one's prior possession by language. And indeed we do see that the speaker's senses are in fact very keen, almost unnaturally so. In a crucial line he says, "My naked ears heard the day pass." In a way, this fascinating line provides the key to the whole poem. It conveys the immediate sense of an extraordinary attentiveness: his ears are completely open to the world (just as in the next line his eyes are "wide open"). But if they are, what do they find? When one thinks of it, the phrase "heard the day pass" can only suggest the perplexed silence of the ear which attempts to hear itself hear or listen to itself listen. Therefore, in addition to the factors we have already enumerated — the prior possession of consciousness by language, and yet its continual exposure to direct experience nonetheless, and the complex intertwining of these two factors, an intertwining in which they perhaps conflict with each other — there is yet a further factor, that of a natural self-reflexivity of sense perception as a conscious process, so that one does not merely hear but is aware of one's hearing, or can become so, one does not merely look but is aware of one's seeing. Consciousness searches in nature for something that will satisfy its desire for meaning; it questions the world, as Merleau-Ponty points out. This questioning, this being in the interrogative mode, may or may not be dependent upon this complex of faculties we are outlining — to say so would imply its dependence on the fact of art, or at least language — yet there is no question that art makes us more aware of this aspect of awareness, of the mind's naturally interrogative character. If it questions continually, what does it ask for? It often seems that it is lured by desire, a desire for *presence*. And yet certainly this is the one thing it cannot find, despite the intensity of sensation which it does experience. Rossetti finds instead the wide silence of the day, an expectant emptiness and a fathomless depth into which Being itself seems to recede — the *apeiron* of pre-Socratic philosophy, of Plato, and of Levinas — and there is as well the pure salience of specific sensation with its inherent *thisness*.

Yet this plenitude and intensity of experience does not really become a surplus. The speaker seems strangely deadened, in fact, and perhaps he is deadened by sensation itself, by its sheer and continually surprising profusion. For, as a general matter, when a certain level of sensation is reached, numbness results and not a Dionysian *excess*. Perhaps it is for this reason, this being numbed through sensation, that he seems to have no real power to act, but is merely pushed along like a dead leaf: "I had walked on at the wind's will. / I sat now, for the wind was still." It is as if perception has been partly detached from the external world; it consolidates a somnambulant state which has become a fulfillment of desire in its own right, one with its own peculiar character and altered sense of duration: the sense of time is slowed subtly in stanzas two and three, so that one has the impression of attention brooding on itself. The movements of consciousness are not quick and alert but hypnotic — despite such bursts of phantasmagoria as the woodspurge flowering "out of the sun" — and the hypnotic effect is increased by the monotonous rhythms and repeated rhymes. There is the suggestion of a loss of time awareness, followed by a partial awakening in the last stanza, and one might ask how long the experience described in the middle stanzas lasts. In spite of the naturalistic detail in such a poem, Rossetti refuses to focus attention on anything other than the inner state of desire and its frustration that is the poem's real subject. He seeks to exclude most of experience, most of its possibilities, despite the details which loom like portents in his gaze, and his listening, despite hearing the day pass, picks up only the internal murmur of the mind itself attempting to live in an alien landscape. And yet this internal murmur is language itself, and its result is the poem.

It is a beautiful piece, moreover. And beauty provides its own satisfactions. Yet the nature of Rossetti's poetry makes one feel that the dense and highly-wrought quality he pursued must be seen as having a significance beyond aesthetic perfection per se. If consciousness is to be estranged from nature, then it must turn to something other than natural experience for its fulfillment; it must turn to this very language itself and to the intangible satisfactions of wielding it. This satisfaction consists partly in a feeling of mastery derived from commanding an uncooperative instrument, but more importantly in the private joy and feeling of confirmation which arises when language itself becomes the object of an almost wholly internalized desire. The desire that remains frustrated elsewhere finds an alternative release in creating a conspicuous style, an intricate and gorgeous weaving of words. The poet himself gives us a clue to this in the introductory sonnet to "The House of Life" sequence. The poem starts with Rossetti's well-known definition of the sonnet as "a moment's monument." The emphasis here is on the word "monument," for he goes on to describe it as a "memorial . . . to one dead deathless hour." Following this comes the central injunction of the poem, the idea that the sonnet — any sonnet — should be written so as to be "Of its own arduous fullness reverent." The placement of the verbal at the end makes the line a kind of circle, since the object of "reverent" — "arduous fullness" — comes before it. In this way a reflexive, self-enfolding gesture is suggested by a phrase that also fills both mouth and ear with complex vowel music. Such a line exemplifies the self-embowering character of Rossetti's art, its pursuit of a state which is heightened and yet self-enclosed and exclusive, and the sonnet which is so opulently monumental is, after all, the memorial of a dead deathless hour.

Borderings

Our discussion has perhaps been overly extensive, yet a surprising amount of Frost's early poetry can be understood in the light of the issues we raise here. It is done in a mode not only stylistically similar to

Rossetti's, but it is also the manifestation of a deep impulse toward reverie and the exclusion of disruptive experience. Yet at an early point in his career, we find him moving beyond such writing by rising to the challenge of those very disruptions. At the same time his work confirms the deeper insight concealed within Rossetti's art — an awareness of the inherent fragility of the self, of the mind, before the flux of nature and the mind's sense of being threatened by this. In his mature work, however, the Good must be found in a context of contingency and in the actual world, as opposed to the privileged inner space of Rossetti's "arduous fullness." In modifying his poetic expression to reflect this, he rejects both the idea of a direct access to things (an idea animating, for example, the work of William Carlos Williams) as well as the idea of a continual play of language and figuration, an orientation often ascribed, say, to Wallace Stevens. He seeks another path, yet it is not one that lies between these. It is entirely other. The way in which it is so is in the awareness that human beings need beauty, both as they find it manifest in the natural world and as they create it themselves. Yet they have an equally strong need for contact with the actual, even though this can be threatening or worse.

This dual desire for beauty and for truth creates in the poet — in this poet — an awareness of what I might call the boundary — the small difference which separates a useful and illuminating metaphor from a fixed and exaggerated distortion. For Frost, just as for Merleau-Ponty, consciousness seems by its nature to be a questioning which yet does not stand over against the external world as an opposed term — consciousness and nature standing opposite each other as antithetical substantives. There is rather a complex intermingling of the two realms, for the mind and the senses are infused with the objects and the circumstances of the world from their first motions, from the earliest phases of their varied and respective actions. There is thus a bordering and liminality inherent in the nature of both. Within *this* context nature and its demands and the mind and its desires are provisionally distinguished and interrelated at once, or rather one should say interwoven. It is this complex act that Frost's style ultimately attempts to represent. Yet in doing so it discovers the continual incipience of change within nature; nature in its own recessed life is constantly on a verge, and yet it is also a mirror in which it shows one that one's own perceptions, indeed one's own faculties likewise are as well — in fleeting impressions and in moods, in the lability of one's attention, one's mind, and in the play of insight and illusion, clarity and obscurity inherent in the metaphors and concepts which organize it. For this reason his style is generally committed to a fluctuating and changeable presentation in which metaphor modifies metaphor and is further nuanced by an encompassing tone — the mimesis of a speaking voice which in its dramatically situated character is itself changing and unstable in its mood and disposition. To glimpse such change, to witness it both without and within, is to become aware of the fluctuating and variable nature of the things of the world in general, and therefore of their vulnerability and exposure. Perhaps only a writer whose imagination was so imbued with the natural world, its organic forms and manifold processes, could summon such tact, such delicacy, and such refinement as we see repeatedly in his work both in its representation of nature and likewise in its handling of human subjects. For this reason it seems to me our way into his poetic world must likewise be by gradations: in order to understand it in its fullness and complexity we must return to follow its progress away from its Romantic starting point one stage at a time.

At the Edge of the Real/Presence and Absence

The poem "Waiting" is an early work included in Frost's first volume, though written probably before the turn of the century. It is a crucial poem there, both for its quality as well as for the way it exemplifies his early style and themes. The superscription "Afield at dusk" locates the poem and provides an imaginative prelude: we are familiar with other poetic fields and with other dusks, so that the opening seems attended by a cloud of poetic ghosts. Yet it is far from overpowered by them, and the speaker perhaps performs a mild rite of exorcism by pointing out that he is alone in the field "From which the laborers' voices late have died." Such deliberate allusiveness indicates the degree to which Frost is aware of his own procedures, aware, in fact, of the literary as a fabric of conventions to be used to further an author's ends, which yet lie beyond those conventions. It is an indication of a lucidity about the nature of poetry and metaphor which one does not always find in a poet like Rossetti, and the presence of which in Frost, as we see it here, gives us some foreshadowing of the sophistication he would eventually attain. It was a sophistication that sought always to control the dangerous powers of metaphor in order to use them to illuminate experience rather than to build protective structures against it. Yet at this stage, it remains a poetry of reverie still, albeit sophisticated and self-aware. The twilight setting, for instance, puts any intrusive elements of the scene at a remove, and even the physicality of the field is subtly altered. To be sure, it is never lost sight of, as the various details show, yet it verges on a

Keatsian or Miltonic lower paradise: a glamour of imagination has been cast over it, so that it appears more posed and poised than any actual landscape could be with its "antiphony of afterglow / And rising full moon." In this slightly charmed context the poet takes up his place. Soon he loses himself, as he tells us, and "dream[s] upon the opposing lights of the hour," which are "Preventing shadow until the moon prevail." The moon is, of course, the symbol of imagination which must be waited on, and which yet does not fully arrive, or has not so far. The speaker, therefore, is suspended between day and dream, between the full presence of actuality which has receded with the setting sun and the complete dominance of the realm of the imagination.[4]

It is precisely this transitional stage he finds most congenial. There is neither nostalgia for the day nor invocation of night; the peculiar charm of twilight serves him well enough. We could say, in fact, that the poem is a meditation on presence and absence in which both are experienced as two different modes of reverie. This can be seen in the way perception is continually diverted toward the non-visual. Sound is prominent, and with it comes hearing's way of drawing the mind into the sound itself, thus altering the flow of consciousness more subtly and pervasively than sight generally can. There is also an important use of the olfactory and a tendency toward synesthesia, both exemplified in a line like "In the abyss of odor and rustle at my back." Such tendencies of style create a context in which what is present is not so clearly present as it might be but is rather slightly veiled by dusk and by the general atmosphere of meditative leisure. In a like manner, absence is experienced not as deprivation but as another thing the poet will "dream upon." Though the woman is absent, her absence is invested with a complex of associations. She becomes an Idea to be apprehended, and since this occurs only in the mind her very absence is made a kind of internal resonance, furnished with evocative tokens. In this way, she takes on a significance which is both more charged and yet simpler than the presence of any actual woman, for she has been turned into a haunting mental object, elusive and yet compelling, a memory seen in the light of past and present desires and now redolent of that remembered and cherished person as though of her essence. Yet at the same time any clear sexual feeling has been sublimed away, in the old alchemical sense, so that all that is left are evocative tokens — a memory, and the penetrating scent of the field. The poem itself is perhaps the last token. Presence and absence are therefore fused in the poem continually and at a variety of levels, so that neither is ever confronted directly. Various critics have demonstrated the allusiveness of the poem's idiom. We might recall that it is sometimes said that allusion is a trope by which is expressed absence in the context of presence and presence in the context of absence. In this case, its use is particularly appropriate, for a wavering apprehension, a shying away from either, is actually the poem's subject.

A brief glance at *A Boy's Will* will suggest a number of other pieces which might also be mentioned here. A consciously "poetic" diction can be seen in a poem like "Rose Pogonias," for example. Richard Poirier makes a telling point when he remarks that at moments the volume seems like a deliberate exercise in Renaissance modes. It is important to emphasize that it is deliberate, though, for the poems exhibit a tremendous control in handling their various conventions. In fact, in the ornamental diction and almost seventeenth-century conceits, one can see a stylistic manifestation of a desire to interpose a barrier of some kind between oneself and experience, in this case through a conscious artificiality and stylized use of language. The poem does, in fact, take the form of a prayer and turns on the idea of a privileged enclosure.[5]

> A saturated meadow,
>   Sun-shaped and jewel-small,
> A circle scarcely wider
>   Than the trees around were tall;
> Where winds were quite excluded,
>   And the air was stifling sweet
> With the breath of many flowers —
>   A temple of the heat.

As this stanza suggests, the poem is an attempt to see a particular place as free of the contingent as likewise of time and its destructions. The poem's conclusion makes this explicit.

> We raised a simple prayer
>   Before we left the spot,
> That in the general mowing
>   That place might be forgot;
> Or if not all so favored,
>   Obtain such grace of hours
> That none should mow the grass there
>   While so confused with flowers.

Something must be preserved, the poem seems to be saying: there must be some respite from the waste of temporality. And yet it is realistic too: it recognizes that such privileged places can exist only in appearance, or only provisionally, at the whim of the unknown god of necessity or chance to which the poem is addressed. This is its modern aspect —

this sense of the provisional — and it is this that will increase in importance as Frost matures. Here, however, it is combined with a diction and rhetoric that are the most deliberately "literary" he ever employed. We could say that the poem represents a compromise: it covertly yields to the temporal, yet in return it demands the self-assertion of a conspicuous style. The invisible wall of language summoned in the first stanza — this braiding of language threaded through with the trope of allusion, of presence in absence, absence in presence, woven of meditations which themselves consider the weight of absence and the lightness of being itself — is a language loved for its own sake and for its origin in a poetic tradition to which the poet has dedicated himself. It creates a mode of incantation by which the mind asserts itself over the mere natural context, though not, it is important to note, in as drastic and potentially dualistic a way as we have seen with Rossetti. It is important to note that here in this piece, or in the previous, the complex textuality does not close off all access to the real and is not intended to. For we see in it at the same time a careful descriptive capacity at work, an eye watching the world, as much as an ear listening to the echoes and resonances of words themselves.

This watching is certainly different from the habits of observation present in, for example, various pieces by William Carlos Williams — "The red wheelbarrow," "as the cat . . . " and others. It is, for instance, not merely visual but inflected by the givens of the other senses: there is a vision influenced by tactile impressions, a haptic sense influenced by scent and by an overall impression of warmth and heat. We realize, as we read, how true it is, as Merleau-Ponty observes, that we do not use our senses singly. Rather we use them together, and they speak to each other and correspond to each other in a complex and mutually influencing permeability. The poem itself is imbued with this unobtrusive syneasthesia. Language itself seems to participate in this, for though it is studied, it is also redolent. Is there not a suggestion of light and of the luminous in the very latinity of some of the words, in the brightness of their sounds and in the sharpness of their syllables? In any event, we may say that Frost could not long have tolerated a poetry of enclosure, even if the enclosures were ones that did implicitly recognize the pressure of the actual as likewise the contingent nature of their own fashioning or for that matter of the tradition — always precious, always endangered — out of which they attempt to weave together beauty itself and gleanings from the world as it is. He must find instead a language more thoroughly imbued with the sense of the contingency of experience, though he takes pains never to give up the beautiful.

Utopian Moments in Time

And yet is beauty still possible for the modern writer, for the modern writer Frost has become once his work internalizes the radical contingency of the world? Or rather, one should perhaps ask, what *kinds* of beauty still are? Is it possible for us still to have a type of writing in which beauty is a primary consideration, both the beauty of language and of form as well as that of nature taken as the subject of representation? Moreover, are we still able to perceive the beauty of nature, to think of it in those terms and to apprehend it in that way? Or is it rather the case that it has receded from us, distanced first by modern biology and physics — two discourses with which Frost was quite familiar — and then by the mere fact of its ongoing crisis, the profound incompatibility between western culture, or at least certain developments in it, and the natural world itself? Frost, it seems to me, had a profound intuition of this incompatibility and of the crisis of both nature and culture that it was bringing about. And yet at the same time he retains, more than almost any other poet of his time and place, the ability to convey moments of idyllic beauty and clarity in which there seems to be no conflict at all between the human world and the natural world and in fact a remarkable harmony. To see this we might turn to one of his more mature idyllic poems. The question it seems to pose is one of balance, as so often in Frost; that is, how to balance the desire for beauty with an awareness of the resistant and unaccommodating nature of the world, and, in particular, how to balance the desire for beauty with a sense of contingency and chance.

THE VALLEY'S SINGING DAY

The sound of the closing outside door was all.
You made no sound in the grass with your footfall,
As far as you went from the door, which was not far;
But you had awakened under the morning star
The first songbird that awakened all the rest.
He could have slept but a moment more at best.
Already determined dawn began to lay
In place across a cloud a slender ray
For prying beneath and forcing the lids of sight,
And loosing the pent-up music of overnight.
But dawn was not to begin their "pearly-pearly"
(By which they mean the rain is pearls so early,
Before it changes to diamonds in the sun),
Neither was song that day to be self-begun.
You had begun it, and if there needed proof —

I was asleep still under the dripping roof,
My window curtain hung over the sill to wet;
But I should awake to confirm your story yet;
I should be willing to say and help you say
That once you had opened the valley's singing day.

"The Valley's Singing Day" is a fine example of Frost's mature approach. We can see that many of the Pre-Raphaelite tendencies have been modified to allow for a more flexible style: there is a more subtle and tonally nuanced use of metaphor, for example, and the tone has been broadened to include an urbane humor. These two factors are connected, since it is by means of tone that the implicit assertion of metaphor is qualified. Nevertheless, and interestingly, the poetry remains concerned with experiences of idyllic embowerment, of the feeling of a rapport between the self and a sensuously heightened natural context. Now, however, this idea is entertained in a fundamentally different way: what is sought is not the "arduous fullness" of Rossetti or his "moment's monument"; but rather a momentary, though undeniable, transformation of experience, a transformation which the poet always recognizes as necessarily transitory. The ability to accept this problem — simultaneous beauty and transience — seems to be inscribed at a deeper level and to manifest itself in a greater number of ways through the whole economy of the text than was seen even in the sophisticated practice of "Rose Pogonias." Artificial durations, slowed time and a self-presence of perception are less pronounced.

In the first three lines the poem is poised between the pull of imagination and a desire to remain rooted in fact. We notice that the sense of hearing is engaged first, the sense which often plays the central role in opening up the realm of the imagination, since it is so closely associated with the powers of reverie and hypnosis. The poet's mind is pulled gently into a state of dream as he listens for the footsteps of this woman (or child?) whom he cannot actually see. The effect is increased by the triple rhythms in the verse which establish a slightly incantatory music. Yet even at the outset, the desire for specificity and fact keeps pace with the initial impulse of dream and prevents it from moving too far from what is immediately perceivable. Thus, the repetition of the word "sound" is balanced by the mention of the outside door, and by the poet's visualizing the entire scene with a certain specificity: "As far as you went from the door, which was not far." The sense of hearing, notoriously vague when it comes to direction, is complemented by the precision of sight whose role is to mark and limit. The consummation of hearing, or rather of listening, is the art of music, an "art of number," as

Valéry puts it, which brings about effortless transformations of experience as the mind is drawn into the dimension of the musical and absorbed within it.[6] Poetry is not music, but there are times when it seeks to be a charm, to throw a qualitative change over represented experience. Yet the poet here seems to feel that this must be counter-balanced by the precise demands of sight, which places the physical world before one in its "thereness," with details and relations clearly marked out, and which naturally compels a respect for the facts such as they are. We see then in this balancing and division of faculties — sight and hearing, ear and eye — a kind of *concordia discors*, that is, a harmonizing of what would be antithetical and conflicting tendencies in the mind, and this for the purpose of allowing the mind an enlarged grasp of the world, one which is attuned to beauty and possibility yet is not delusory.

At the same time we do not see the synaesthesia-like fusion into a kind of massed sensorium which was a feature of the earlier work. Ear and eye share the scene and divide it; they complement and enlarge the grasp of the real, yet they do not blur together. There is thus a greater discreteness of perception and a corresponding clarity. The poem works through acts of balancing rather than attempted fusions or exclusions. Indeed the idea of a *concordia discors* is familiar, of course, from eighteenth-century aesthetics, where it betokened a well-tempered style, indeed a well-tempered imagination, one shunning extravagance and exaggeration. Invoking it in this context reminds one of the significant connection Frost's aesthetic always maintained with neo-classical values of balance, decorum, and avoidance of excess. Yet at the same time, he remains a modern poet, and this is shown above all in the importance given to sense impressions in general in his writing, and beyond that, the implied importance of these impressions, and of the senses themselves, in the life of human beings and thus for the imagination itself in its attempt to create an image of happiness.

It is important to note that there was a sort of movement to avoid sense perception in American poetry at around this time. Yvor Winters, for instance, repeatedly expressed a distrust of sense impressions in poetry, and the relentlessly abstract language which, for a while, became fashionable — in work by Ransom, Tate, and others — exhibited also a suspicion of sense impressions in literary style. Yet Frost seems to have instinctively understood the anachronistic and reactionary character of this approach and its inevitable failure. The capacity for sense description, so carefully developed through the eighteenth and nineteenth centuries, was a profound achievement of culture that could not simply be discarded. Moreover, and more importantly, how can an image of happiness be created which ignores the physical embodiment of human beings? And how can there be a major body of literature which does not have, as one of its bases, the creation of such an image?

Thus the poem continues with an atmospheric description, actually a suggestion, of landscape:

> But you had awakened under the morning star
> The first songbird that awakened all the rest.
> He could have slept but a moment more at best.

From one standpoint, these lines are completely factual: a woman has gone out onto the lawn in the early morning, and the sound of the door shutting behind her has awakened the sleeping birds. But an element of romance is present as well. There is again the element of the triple rhythms and a *sotto voce* tone, so that as one thinks of it the image of a woman on the lawn listening to the just-awakened birds acquires a mysterious, haunting quality and perhaps an element of pathos. The mention that this occurs "under the morning star" only deepens the suggestiveness. In such a passage we are not far from Wordsworth who liked to imagine privileged moments of rapport with the natural world. In the first two lines one can hear an echo of the closing benediction of "Tintern Abbey," or the similar gesture at the end of Coleridge's "Frost at Midnight." It is a moment in which the human world and nature achieve a delicate reciprocity. Yet such an experience can never be extended beyond its proper moment. Therefore the significance Frost derives from it will not become a principle of renewal working through his whole being, as Wordsworth would attempt to imagine it, and he refrains from building up greatest things from least suggestions. It is rather a single moment of inherent excellence, as Stevens might put it, and we see that, characteristically, the passage is qualified by the playful and yet quiet humor of the very next line.

This ingratiating quality is continued in lines seven through ten, as the poet describes the dawn light awakening the birds and "loosing the pent-up music of overnight." The tone of the remaining ten lines, however, is more difficult to characterize, for they are not merely playful, and still less are they limited to the clearly factual. It is an odd tone — one that would half-persuade us of the marvelous, almost in the sense given to that word by the Surrealists themselves — evoking, that is, moments of fortuitous beauty of an uncanny and unearthly kind, moments which take us out of our normal awareness, perhaps by a subtle adjustment of perception or a slight distancing of the real. Yet it is a tone that also, and equally, demands that we remain ultimately skeptical, aware of the burden of time and mortality that lies hidden in every moment of vision. It is perhaps the voice of innocence and experience simultaneously.

What demands can such a passage make on us, or we on it and its inherently ambiguous style — a shifting, somewhat elusive poetry whose central figures may have an unsettled and existentially disengaged character? Some clarification of its purpose in this context can be found in Geoffrey Hartman's treatment of Wordsworth, and in particular his handling of "The Solitary Reaper." Hartman points out that Wordsworth's poem can be seen as a fabric of surmise, which he defines as the mind's capacity to entertain various imaginative possibilities in order to comprehend experience, without definitely settling on any one interpretation. As Hartman explains, "Surmise is fluid in nature; it likes 'whether . . . or' formulations, alternatives rather than exclusions, echoing conjecture (Keats' "Do I wake or sleep?") rather than blunt determinateness. The actual is in some ways the potential. . . . "[7] Surmise is therefore a way of opening up experience rather than limiting it, of clarifying it without attempting to determine its significance with premature definiteness. It is a questioning of the world as much as a description of it and seems related to Merleau-Ponty's idea of "being in the interogative mode." It should not be understood as evasion, but as a more inclusive mode of perception. Yet it is clear that a certain detachment is needed as a prerequisite. Surmise, therefore, has the effect of distancing things, of placing them at an aesthetic remove: they lose some of their urgency, yet the mind is liberated to move among possibilities. Surmise offers itself as a way of representing experience that will violate neither it nor the speaker: it is rational and yet not reducible to rationalism, and in this way it provides the possibility for a balance between mind, selfhood, and desire and the realities of an imperfectly known, imperfectly knowable world. The mind presses its claim for meaning yet refrains from doing so too strenuously lest both it and nature suffer. As Hartman puts it of Wordsworth:

> The essential fact is that Wordsworth allows the sudden emotion (or, in the daffodil poem, sudden optical impression) to invade and renew his mind instead of reducing the emotion by an act of mind. Knowing that his relation to nature is as unpredictable as a relation of Grace — that whether or not he originally responded and whether or not he responded fully, the encounter has a secret life that may later flash out and renew his feelings — Wordsworth adopts the stance of surmise which points to liberty and expansiveness of spirit. (*Wordsworth's Poetry* 9)

Hartman's Wordsworth attends to possibilities which are inherent in a charged and numinous landscape. For Frost, the reality of nature is perhaps less inspiring. Yet it will not do to say that for him nature is terrible. It would be more correct to say that it has receded in the wake of modern skepticism. And yet only to a point. Nature is enigmatic and can only be reached through partial acts of perception, of divinations through metaphor and description. Yet as physical reality it is continually present and continually imposes demands that affect us in the most concrete ways. It faces us as a paradox, for it is both elusive and inassimilable to any metaphor while yet pressing urgent and imperative demands upon us. The mental act which Hartman calls surmise is perfectly suited to such a circumstance, since it recognizes the claims of both immediate perception with its urgencies and a broader, encompassing uncertainty. At the same time, it encourages both an imaginative participation in the reality of present experience and a recognition of hidden or enigmatic realities which may be latent in it. Perhaps we might also relate such an idea to Keats's Negative Capability, his "ideal capacity" to be in "uncertainties, mysteries, doubts, without any irritable reaching after fact and reason. . . ."[8] The ultimate provenance of Frost's style from both Keats and Wordsworth is evident, therefore, not only at more obvious stylistic levels but at this subtle conceptual level too. Hartman's Wordsworth must suspend judgment, just as Keats also knows one must do. Frost performs a similar act of partial liberation. In the last ten lines of "The Valley's Singing Day" we see the poet summoning such a moment of natural enchantment which yet is aware of the dark penumbra which surrounds it. He possesses a kind of willingness to be charmed and asks the same of us while all the time exhibiting a sophisticated tolerance of the unpredictable and the contingent: the exquisiteness and fragility of the poem are a tacit acknowledgment of the realities of time, chance, and mortality, the dark substratum on which it floats like a leaf on the surface of a deep pool.

The Sovereign Other

In a similar way, Frost's "The Silken Tent" is a poem that deals with desire in the context of the contingency of the world. Contingency, of course, implies a lack of control on the part of the subject (in this case the speaker of the poem). Yet in this instance it is a lack of control over the Other — a lack of control, of domination, which the speaker must acknowledge and be willing to acknowledge and affirm for ethical reasons. At the same time, it is a fact which he must recognize for intellectual reasons as well; to fail to do so would be to remain in a deluded state regarding the relationship of self and world, or in this case self and Other.

The poem is remarkably elaborate and takes the form of a graduated unfolding. The fact that it is a sonnet and also a single continuous sentence contributes to this impression. We witness the completion of a thought, the dawning of a realization, as it moves through the obstacles created by the sonnet form itself, slowed by them and given a deliberateness — a celebratory deliberateness, as we might think of it, as though the speaker did not want to go too fast but sought to remain suspended in this moment of rapt and yet sober recognition.

THE SILKEN TENT

She is as in a field a silken tent
At midday when a sunny summer breeze
Has dried the dew and all its ropes relent,
So that in guys it gently sways at ease,
And its supporting central cedar pole,
That is its pinnacle to heavenward
And signifies the sureness of the soul,
Seems to owe naught to any single cord,
But strictly held by none, is loosely bound
By countless silken ties of love and thought
To everything on earth the compass round,
And only by one's going slightly taut
In the capriciousness of summer air
Is of the slightest bondage made aware.

This oddness of metaphor, aside from creating a continual expectancy and an ongoing surprise, also diverts any descriptive impulse the speaker might have had. The Beloved is characterized in her fundamental nature, but she is never described. One might see this absence of direct description as preserving her from the intrusion and appropriation which any direct representation amounts to. She exceeds the possibility of description. In Merleau-Ponty the exceeding of a perception by further perception, of aspect by further aspects in the exploration of an object, is part of the basic nature of perception and is caused by the fact that the world continually exceeds any view I have of it and which it occasions me to have or any concept I develop. This same idea of an object exceeding one's conception of it or one's expectations is applied by Levinas to persons and is the basis for his ethical insight that the Other is radically other and cannot be viewed as a sort of variant of myself.[9] The Other challenges me and limits my freedom by implicitly contesting any descriptions I might make of him or her, exceeding them in an always unpredictable newness and "welling up." The poem is a rather static and pictorial piece for Frost, but a similar intuition of the separation and inherent transcendence of the Other is implied in it. She is shown to exceed the speaker's desires and expectations in the very fact that she is not described. She does not have to do anything to bring this about; this exceeding is not the product of her action or speech. It is implied in her very nature. The poem implicitly acknowledges this in its very first line as we have already noted. It merely says, *she is*. It is a statement as simple as it is dignified.[10] The dignity we appreciate only by degrees, the careful process of the poem that is a single sentence. Yet the simplicity of such an assertion puzzles one at first, and we may be tempted to look for a subject complement which surely, we feel, must be coming. She is what? But no, she merely is, and that is enough. Just as Merleau-Ponty speaks of discovering facets, aspects in a process of questioning the world, a being in the interrogative mode, likewise here her being is revealed gradually in a slow process of discovery. It is a process that continually surprises, since it reveals what exceeds one's expectations — her being as such and her otherness.

This exceeding is conveyed through the rather far-fetched quality of the conceit itself: she is, in the same way that in a field a silken tent . . . One might not have thought to compare a woman to a tent, silken or otherwise, yet point by point and moment by moment one is continually surprised at its aptness, an aptness the poet himself seems to discover even as we do, an appropriateness made manifest to us and in a sense created by a combined rhetorical daring and circumspection. Her reality cannot be encompassed by normal comparisons, or indeed by any, and yet one must make the attempt, lured on in one's effort at expression by a kind of imperative that her existence places upon one, by the desire the relationship to her creates, and also by her absolute otherness in relation to the speaker, an otherness which in its absoluteness can never be bridged, yet which provides the space for her appearance itself, for her sovereign manifestation as a desired object and for this very desire which can only exist within the space of that separation, and which somehow constitutes it, determining it as a rapt and unavoidable inclination and yet also as a solicitude which must deny itself at precisely the point where it would make of her an object (for this is the one thing she cannot be). She is and must always be rather the sovereign Other to whom the speaker is yet connected by countless silken ties, the expressions of the profound and mutual attunement of two natures, that of man and of woman. Therefore if even the speaker's desire, which, in the context of the poem, and in the context of its genre — the love sonnet, and a rather Petrarchan one in feeling despite its Shakespearean form

— is almost his very being itself, cannot reach to her in a way definitive enough to make of her an object, even if it be the object of the most exalted and purest of desires — and it is a very exalted poem, and this is, of course, its Petrarchan dimension — then surely no mere effort at verbal expression, at comparison can either. There can be no *adaequatio.* And so the poet chooses this rather improbable and slightly biblical conceit, allowing its very distance from her, its unlikeness on the level of empirical observation, to be the space, the infinite and strangely subtle, and strangely resonant space of its expression, its observance of her, of its simultaneous knowledge and non-comprehension. And here its biblical resonance — pointed out by Richard Poirier — becomes appropriate, for there can be no doubt that he does have knowledge of her in the biblical sense, as we sometimes facetiously say. Yet here these two dimensions — the biblical dedication of embodied personhood and the Petrarchan access to the Platonic realm of light, an element in which the poem is permeated — are balanced against each other, so that the poem does not incline either to a specifically sexual vision nor to an idealizing one, but includes both and surpasses even the combination of the two in a vision of otherness which cannot be limited to either.

We will return to this idea of balance and balancing, another *concordia discors* shortly, but before we do it is necessary to complete the description we are building of the ways the poem even in its high aestheticism maintains a sense of the Beloved's otherness, of the fact that she cannot be assimilated to any of the metaphors or descriptions which the poet shows himself so eminently capable of, nor defined by his rhetoric. Perhaps for this reason Levinas might after all be the inevitable theorist to invoke, for his philosophy is perhaps the greatest example of a profound fusion of the two different cultural inheritances we see mingled here — the Hellenic and the Hebraic, to use Arnold's terminology. Thus we must attend to the ways the poem in its very efforts at tribute, celebration, and oblique description deliberately diverted into baroque complication, itself attends to the otherness, the continual exteriority of the Beloved. We recall that in Levinas the Beloved is virginal and inviolate in her nature:

> The Beloved, at once graspable but intact in her nudity, beyond object and face and thus beyond the existent, abides in virginity. The feminine essentially violable and inviolable, the "Eternal Feminine," is the virgin or an incessant recommencement of virginity (*Totality* 258)

As we have suggested, the poem's very formality, with its cultivated indirectness displayed in both metaphor and in syntax, itself conveys this.

Yet what of the speaker's desire? Does he cede it, as Lacan repeatedly warned we must not? Is it sufficient to invoke an idea of sublimation, as we in part did at the outset of this chapter in discussing what we there called the libidinal investment in a type of language?

The central metaphor is designed to convey a sense of how the seemingly contradictory ideas of fulfillment and limitation, desire and constraint, are interrelated and often imply each other. Similarly, the *I* (the interior world from which this desire originates) and the externality surrounding it — and so too the sovereignty of desire, and the contingency and otherness which contest that sovereignty — exist in a reciprocal and subtly interactive relationship, and not merely in an antagonistic one. The poem conveys this by its very design; as many have pointed out, it is a sonnet which is also a continuous sentence, a sentence which articulates its central metaphor with a metaphysical elaboration — though in a manner which seems completely effortless. Frost's willingness to be so formally constrained is indicative of his willingness to be bound in other ways. His imagination accepts the limitations imposed on human aspirations by time, circumstance, and the natural world. In fact he willingly embraces them, and even insists on them. Thus we might say that he saw the possibility for fulfillment in either art or life as existing only in the context of resistance and limit imposed by the world. He did not, however, view this with melancholy but celebrated it as providing a sharper incentive to the creative will, which can truly grow only through encountering such external and alien entanglements.

Therefore nature is allowed to enter the texture of the writing not as mere *exempla* but as a determining context, for though it may be true that the conceit of the poem uses the images of field and breeze, of cedar pole and of encompassing light and warmth, these images themselves are not merely rhetorical ones. Rather they are conveyed with deft descriptive touches, a tact which itself refrains from merely appropriating them, but allows them their independent and living existence as inassimilable things in the world, as nourishing, supporting elements, as elementals in Levinas's sense.[11] These are presented as gleanings, perhaps, hints and brief glimpses. And yet it is enough to create the sense of concreteness that we see in the poem, despite its deliberate artifice; we notice an apparent desire to remain in contact with things that has not been impaired by the elaboration of syntax and conceit. There is a concern with situation and occasion, with apprehending a particular moment in an actual field. Of course, the situation is not specific: the poem does not have an overt dramatic context, yet it is imbued with a sense of the physical, of sexuality, and of the ways these impinge upon an individual. We see this clearly in the presence of the physical realities — light, field, breeze, the vibrant day itself. It is not an overwhelming presence, and in fact is more obliquely presented than in many of Frost's other poems. Yet it pervades the writing nonetheless, both as a general atmosphere of warmth and light and as an array of images. The poem is engaged in balancing the things of the mind — metaphor, desire itself in fact — with the facts of the world, and we come to realize that such balancing is its ultimate concern: desire, though it must be fulfilled for a truly human life, can gain this fulfillment only by working in the midst of the concrete actualities of the world, which are the inevitable resistance it must take into account, the unavoidable weight it must bear, lightly if possible. We might compare this balancing of real but opposed burdens with a similar moment in Valéry in which the complexities of selfhood and the weight of the world, of the external, are reconciled in a single vibrant image of poise:

Pour autant qu'elle se plie
À l'abondance des biens,
Sa figure est accomplie,
Ses fruits lourds sont ses liens.
Admire comme elle vibre,
Et comme une lente fibre
Qui divise le moment,
Départage sans mystère
L'attirance de la terre
Et le poids du firmament![12]

"L'abondance des biens" and the "fruits lourds" are simultaneously burdens and blessings, just as are selfhood and sexuality and their context of relations in the world. Though Frost speaks elsewhere of the will braving alien entanglements, in his idyllic mode of which "The Silken Tent" is a consummate example we find him completely at home in such entanglements, such "liens," and even welcoming them. And just as Valéry's palm remains poised between the attraction of the earth and the weight of heaven, giving each its due and balancing the two claims with equilibrium and equanimity, so the inspiring and circumscribing conditions of the sunny summer breeze (certainly a romantic breath of spirit) and the thousand silken ties have their ultimate issue in the central cedar pole balanced between heaven and earth.

Conclusion: The Origin of a Style and the Fragility of Nature

The importance of Frost's early poetry lies in its indication of two or three salient points. The first is that we must recognize that for him there really is no plain style: there is only style. His mature style is marked at its source by the pictorial, by synesthesia, by the literary in general. Its frequent transparencies are modifications of an inherent lushness and sensuality. It is a lushness, moreover, which begins in reverie, a mode in which consciousness attempts to defend itself against the surprising and the disruptive. His work moves away from that specific mode without giving up a crucial investment in sense experience, and an equally crucial investment in beauty and form, in the traditional languages of poetry. Resistance to Frost comes as much from a sense of his lushness and pictorial quality as from anything else. Yet he himself has a certain ambivalence about the stylization of his own language, not because he thinks that plain is better, but because he has a concern for the specificity of the world. In the partial revealing and concealing of the things themselves which language and metaphor give us, we glimpse not merely the limitations of our language and our concepts before a reality which always exceeds them but also something else: our own capacity to distort those things, to deform that reality. Yet this potential for distortion does not mean merely that we as humans fall into falsehood and illusion. It means also that these things in their reality are subject to our language, to our metaphors, and in a sense are vulnerable before them. For we act in the world according to our metaphors and imagine things according to our language. Yet the actions undertaken on such a basis are not always wise and our imagination not necessarily motivated by a desire for truth but by desire itself. The fragility of the world consists of two things, therefore. The first is its subtle complexity, a subtlety and a complexity which cannot be done justice to by a plain, self-denying style but only by the style which exhibits in its very figurative ambiguities a being-in-the-interrogative-mode as this applies to human perception itself and to the world in its flux and lability, for the world too is comprised of what is unfixed and in process just as perception itself is. Frost's style in its mature form aims to exhibit the interrogative nature of both the subject inquiring and of the objective world itself. Both exist in an unfixed and questioning state. Both are fluctuating and vulnerable to an incipient change which burgeons within them.

And yet the second factor is that the world contains human beings who are free to interrogate it and to develop metaphorical constructs based on what they find in it, the validity of which as guides to either thought or action cannot be guaranteed. Moreover our development of these constructs and our expression of these desires is constitutive of what we are; it is not optional. There is never a time when we step outside this system, this capacity; we are never outside of desire, of language, or of metaphor. Just as there is never a time when Frost's style attempts to be completely "plain." Yet in its peculiar delicacy and accuracy, its exquisite word sense and cultivated transparency it does allow this plight to be seen. For even in its most reverie-laden mode, the details of existence and especially of organic life — the salient life of leaf and stem, grass blade and flower petal — show through, as it were, and are presented in their delicacy and specificity. The grain of the wood, the grain of the world, is always apparent, even here, and will become more so still as his style reaches its most subtle adjustments in its full maturity.

Yet the style is itself a contrivance, driven by desire for beauty and equally a desire for truth: the first requires a traditional richness, the second a flexibility whether on the level of image, metaphor, or tone, or some combination of these. A plain style, would not be sufficient for his purposes, because it does not acknowledge sufficiently its own fictionality. Moreover, it cannot do justice to the merely human side of this complex situation, the plight of the world. For this plight consists in this very human presence, which must itself be understood and not elided in a supposed objectivism. This understanding cannot take place if desire itself is ignored. This is one of the most important reasons for Frost's formalism. It is not that writing free verse is a game made too easy — tennis with the net down. It is rather that there is a libidinal investment in form, in these traditional forms, in fact, and in the beautiful language which they tend to call forth. Beauty itself must always be present if the human with all its complex desires, these desires which drive it and torment it, is to be understood and adequately presented. It is not merely that the aspirations of characters *in situ* in the poems must be presented in their psychology; but it must also be that the reader himself or herself must have his or her desires addressed, and these are always desire for what is beautiful, even if this itself is repressed, as it is in many versions of modernism and post-modernism. Yet there is inescapably a libidinal investment in form, in clear description and in fascinating metaphors which speaks to a deep and inescapable involvement with the world. It is this wanting to see (the world), this wanting to hear (the harmony of language made manifest), this *wanting more* which must be addressed in the reader if the reality of the human in the world is to be presented in its true complexity.

There is even a utopian impulse present here, for this wanting to see, to hear, this wanting more is a utopian desire inscribed deeply within the human mind and inescapably characteristic of it. It dreams of the beautiful and of a life characterized by beauty; it dreams of a felicity in history, both personal and collective, a dream from which it in fact can never escape. Can the world in its nature support such dreams? This is one of the fundamental question of Frost's work, one which brings it into a strange and historically hidden dialogue with that of Ernst Bloch, for example. I feel that Frost's ultimate response to this question is negative. And yet it is remarkable how so often through so much of his writing life he is willing to allow this utopian desire to express itself quite simply in the form of beauty. It is ironic that his work was dismissed by the American Marxist left at that time, for he was giving expression to a utopian impulse in history through the very style and form of his work, a utopian desire they might have made critical use of, if they had been aware of it. And yet they were blinded by its very grace and clarity, and deafened by its harmonious expression. Yet the beauty of Frost's style is not perhaps, finally, the promise of happiness, but rather the showing forth of a task, the attempt to live in the world.

CHAPTER TWO

The Poetry of Education

Repetition and Discovery

"Birches" is one of those poems that are too well known. Like a number of Frost's pieces it has suffered too much the contamination of anthologies and kept poor company in numerous grade-school textbooks. Such a circumstance heightens our awareness of its shortcomings, at times a slight sentimentality or the too self-conscious charm of certain passages. Yet it is a beautiful poem, one that lingers in the memory and calls us to the task of rereading it.

The poem opens with a gesture which will prove typical of the whole: an initial "realistic" observation is followed by an overtly figurative complement.

> When I see birches bend to left and right
> Across the lines of straighter darker trees,
> I like to think some boy's been swinging them.

Here the far-fetched quality of the metaphor is such that it demands an immediate adjustment: a note of fancifulness is evident and must be corrected lest the poem float off into mere fantasy. "But swinging doesn't bend them down to stay/As ice storms do." This pattern is a familiar one in Frost; it seeks a balance between imagination and the factual and might be seen as an enlargement of the *concordia discors* discussed in the last chapter with respect to mental faculties. Now it is expanded to include the entire person as he or she moves among the objects and purposes of the world. Yet this strategy, to be genuine, must not be accomplished too easily. And perhaps a somewhat facile note has been struck so far, to some extent (as for some it might have been in "The Valley's Singing Day"). There needs to be significant resistance for mind and body to work against. We notice, therefore, that once the ice storms make their appearance they cannot be merely dismissed. In fact the poem seems to lose its way for a moment, to wander into a discourse on storms and their aftermath. Yet even here the same strategy persists;

the poetry is poised between the alternatives of Desire and Necessity and seems to mediate between them:

> Often you must have seen them
> Loaded with ice a sunny winter morning
> After a rain. They click upon themselves
> As the breeze rises, and turn many-colored
> As the stir cracks and crazes their enamel.
> Soon the sun's warmth makes them shed crystal shells
> Shattering and avalanching on the snow crust —
> Such heaps of broken glass to sweep away
> You'd think the inner dome of heaven had fallen.
> They are dragged to the withered bracken by the load,
> And they seem not to break; though once they are bowed
> So low for long, they never right themselves:
> You may see their trunks arching in the woods
> Years afterwards, trailing their leaves on the ground
> Like girls on hands and knees that throw their hair
> Before them over their heads to dry in the sun.

The poetry exhibits a very strong desire to keep opposites balanced against each other. Thus, despite its beauty, this passage is a meditation on loss, the loss concealed in the midst of the beauty and possibility of the world. The inner dome of heaven has fallen, the poet tells us; nonetheless, he creates not an image of terror but of enchantment: the world become a glittering realm of crystal poured out at our feet. This is indeed the very image of the possible, of enchantment itself, perhaps of a kind only available in youth. Yet still, in the midst of this, we must recognize that some things "never right themselves." It is a moment of slight pathos, broken off immediately by another beguiling figure, that of girls throwing their hair before them to dry in the sun. For a moment we seem to be back in the Pre-Raphaelite world. But what is the function of such a simile in this context? Does it mitigate the pathos by means of a Keatsian echo, idyllic and redolent of the harvest of natural happiness (the harvest of "To Autumn" as she is personified "sitting careless on a granary floor," her hair "soft lifted by the winnowing wind")? Or does it deepen pathos by suggesting an association between the trees bowed low and young girls who one day will also be, though now they cannot realize this? Rather than choose we might consider it a pivotal detail, one that opens on two opposed worlds: that of fulfilled desire, and that of experience with its reality of loss. In this way the poem attempts to actually fuse a vision of idyllic innocence with a more realistic one, to mediate between the two and to allow awareness itself to be momentarily stretched taut between them, as the threads of the silken tent were stretched taut in the erotic desire which yet could not reach across the absolute separation between two persons. Thus if the passage quoted possesses a perceptible undercurrent of loss, the succeeding lines seem to present a small myth of aspiration and its capacity to realize itself in the world. It is an enterprise that requires both poise and boldness (or even transgression). In fact, we might see it as remarkable for its Wordsworthian quality, for though it is rather dream-like, it conveys a strong sense of what I can only call athleticism — buoyant energy, youthfulness, and a happy self-abandon, all feelings like those expressed in the opening books of the *Prelude.* In this case such feelings are celebrated as the manifestation of desire and its satisfaction, and they provide the essential motive of the poem — the conviction that desire must be fulfilled if one is to become fully human, but that in the process it is still necessary to deal with the actual world and its contingencies and loss. Yet is it possible to fuse these two things — desire and the overcoming of obstacles, making of desire a self-actualizing power, and of obstacles beckoning lures and horizons?

> But I was going to say when Truth broke in
> With all her matter of fact about the ice storm,
> I should prefer to have some boy bend them
> As he went out and in to fetch the cows —
> Some boy too far from town to learn baseball,
> Whose only play was what he found himself,
> Summer or winter, and could play alone.
> One by one he subdued his father's trees
> By riding them down over and over again
> Until he took the stiffness out of them,
> And not one but hung limp, not one was left
> For him to conquer. He learned all there was
> To learn about not launching out too soon
> And so not carrying the tree away
> Clear to the ground. He always kept his poise
> To the top branches, climbing carefully
> With the same pains you use to fill a cup
> Up to the brim, and even above the brim.
> Then he flung outward, feet first, with a swish,
> Kicking his way down through the air to the ground.

At least as far as this passage is concerned, the answer would seem to be yes. Frost does not have the reputation of being a poet who celebrates human desire in any of its forms, yet the need for it to be satisfied on all levels is one of the main concerns of his work, and, as I was attempting to show in the previous chapter, one of the main reasons for the concern with beauty in his stylistic practices. "Birches," at any rate, is entirely on the side of desire, wanting to fill its cup to the brim "and even above the brim"; only as an acknowledgment of practical necessity does it traffic in ideas of limit. We realize now that perhaps the awareness of loss suggested in the first passage can be seen as a kind of clearing of the ground, a ritual of preparation so that the ensuing myth of aspiration might be more convincingly entertained. The strange sexual and oedipal overtones are therefore not out of place, though they must also not be allowed to dominate one's response to the poem too much. Yet they illustrate both the depth of the desire we refer to here, and the fact that it does indeed include the sexual even in its most direct manifestations; they also show that this desire cannot achieve its own fulfillment unopposed, but that there is always a prior context against which it must strive.

From a stylistic standpoint, the flexibility and elusiveness of Frost's style is seen here to good advantage, as it gives a kind of verbal enactment of the changes and qualifications of expression needed to track the changing manifestations of desire.

> I'd like to go by climbing a birch tree,
> And climb black branches up a snow-white trunk
> *Toward* heaven, till the tree could bear no more,
> But dipped its top and set me down again.

This is not an epigram, and yet we can see how syntax and grammar function as the *incipits* of an entire metaphoric system. The conditional mood, for instance, is itself expressive of a desire, an aspiration which moves counter to fact, and so much so that the verb (to climb) is repeated around the corner, the turning of a single line. It is repeated therefore and emphasized and yet also delayed, deferred, perhaps by a beat or a breath. The verb itself announces the basic metaphor — climbing birch trees — so that it is like the root of a system which will proliferate through the poem, sometimes keeping closer to realism in its mode of imagistic expression, sometimes becoming outrightly fanciful, indeed almost surreal, or seeming to approach the allegorical. A fairly candid desire and an elaborate system of tropes are entangled from the beginning in such a way that the latter will almost certainly have to be modified in any number of ways, and if they are it only indicates the modifications that desire itself must undergo, the complexity of its instantiation in the world. Yet aspiration is not necessarily put aside in irony. We might rather see it as renewed in a desire for contact with the actual. It is this which brings about the poem's various images of touching down, setting down, of coming back to earth — we see the repeated suggestion of a renewal of attempt and inauguration as such, of setting out as such, of beginning. For it is this which is the clearest expression of desire as it encounters the real against which it works, into which it launches itself in quest, exploration, and curiosity. In that experience of beginning, dream and reality are poised against each other without conflict, or rather they are interleaved and seem to exist as one, the tension between them seeming not to be one of incompatibles but rather of complementary forces working together, as muscles work with and against each other in well-coordinated movement. Indeed the poem is about movement as much as anything, and the dream it conveys is a much more active and even restless one than the static and stilled moments we have seen so far. It is rather a power and a motivation (and it is one of the peculiarities of the poem that it makes us feel this experience, of dream as *energy and power*, rather than as escape). The passage, therefore, expresses a desire for a continually renewed *first time.* This, of course, can never literally be the case. But it can be the case in a virtual sense, if experience and actions are thought of in the right way and if actions are then undertaken in the right way. The virtuality of metaphor empowers the mind by conferring a degree of freedom, the freedom of the hypothetical. Yet there is an innate need for the real which brings one continually back to actual experience itself. The pattern of the poem, then, is one of metaphor followed by qualification and adjustment which is at every point imbued with a certain pragmatic shrewdness and a sense of concrete experience and effort (albeit a fresh one, unencumbered by fatigue). Desire and necessity are the poles between which the piece moves in its endeavor to gain both insight and poise, which, by this point, the poem has persuaded us to define as a kind of cultivated balance in the ongoing risk and venture of exploration and self-exploration. This process is not exactly play (or not merely that), and we notice that the boy in the poem, the archetypal Youth, does not play, or even learn, baseball. And yet it certainly is not work. How then to characterize it? Going and coming back can only be types of repetition, yet a creative repetition such as we find expounded by Deleuze, in his work *Difference and Repetition,* in which the latter is essentially a power of creativity and renewal, a creatively and self-renewing engagement with the specificity of the things of the world. To create differences out of repetition is to create novelty where there might be stasis; likewise to gather repetition from difference is to cultivate the coherence and continuity that are needed as a background for the creative. To be capable of these two feats together is to have a power, specifically, the power that prevents life from being either too little or too much — too little in the sense of an impoverished and monotonous expanse in which one can find little of value, or too much in the sense of an overwhelming power that subdues and destroys one's capacity for creativity and responsiveness.[1] The poem is therefore about power — or, to use a more Frostian word, *prowess.* It is the power to make use of time. Time must be imagined as that which enables us to return to a given thing or context which yet itself is never the same, even at any given moment, and to redirect a renewed power of involvement into it, a power and a process which result in further powers, further process, all always self-differentiated and yet productive, building upon themselves in a never entirely foreseeable creation of novelty in Whitehead's sense, a creative process, non-chaotic yet burgeoning in a renewed sameness and renewed *haeccaeity.* In this way, the present stands out from the future and past, and the flow of time is rendered consistent though not uniform, periodic though not monotonous, and unpredictable though not chaotic. We might call such a power, or congregation of powers drawn forth by things out of ourselves and by ourselves out of things and circumstances, repetition forward (as opposed to the repetition in one place of industrial production or mere habit), though another and more mundane term for it would simply be learning, for in learning one takes what is foreign into oneself, learns how to combine it with oneself and oneself with it, and learns also by this means new rhythms, new durations, and new temporal vistas, perhaps those opened up by an activity, a scientific discourse, or a work of art and its relevant traditions.

Yet the positive power of repetition imagined by both Deleuze and Frost does not occur in a completely hospitable realm. It is not for nothing that it is common to speak of Frost's dark side, and Alain Badiou is correct to point to a fundamental asceticism in Deleuze himself.[2] The thought of repetition arises from the ground of adversity — not from the ground of lack, *manque,* or "absence" — but from the positive adversity of active suffering or the actual resistance of physical objects, or of one's own body, to one's will and desires. "Every poem is an epitome of the great predicament; a figure of the will braving alien entanglements." The value of such entanglements is that they engage one with something external to oneself and call forth the deepest energies of imagination and will. We might recall one of Frost's prose statements on this theme:

> The background in hugeness and confusion shading away from where we stand into black and utter chaos; and against the background any small man-made figure of order and concentration. What pleasanter than that

this should be so? Unless we are novelists or economists we don't worry about this confusion; we look out on it with an instrument or tackle it to reduce it. It is partly because we are afraid it might prove too much for us and our blend of democratic-republicansocialist-communistanarchist party. But it is more because we like it, we were born to it, born used to it and have practical reasons for wanting it there. To me any little form I assert upon it is velvet, as the saying is, and to be considered for how much more it is than nothing. If I were a Platonist I should have to conconsider it, I suppose, for how much less it is than everything. (*Selected Prose* 107)

"But it is more because we like it, we were born to it, born used to it and have practical reasons for wanting it there." This is certainly the most striking sentence in the (somewhat blustery) passage. And it is clearly one which illustrates his known kinship with Thoreau and Emerson, particularly with the harshness of the latter's essay "Experience." Yet, again, we may find parallels with Keats, the Keats who realizes the need to pass beyond the Chamber of Maiden Thought (his own term for the embowered imagination) into the Vale of Soul Making:

Do you not see how necessary a World of Pains and troubles is to school an intelligence and make it a Soul? A Place where the heart must feel and suffer in a thousand diverse ways! Not merely is the Heart a Hornbook, It is the Minds Bible, it is the mind experience, it is the teat from which the Mind or intelligence sucks its identity. As various as the lives of Men are — so various become their Souls, and thus does God make individual beings . . . If what I have said should not be plain enough, as I fear it may not be, I will put you in the place where I began in this series of thoughts — I mean, I began by seeing how man was formed by circumstances — and what are circumstances? — but touchstones of his heart? — and what are touchstones? but provings of his heart? and what are provings of his heart but fortifiers or alterers of his nature? and what is his altered nature but his soul? — and what was his soul before it came into the world and had these provings and alterations and perfectionings? — An intelligence — without Identity — and how is this Identity to be made? Through the medium of the heart? And how is the heart to become the Medium but in a world of Circumstances?[3]

In a way these remarks importantly clarify the vision set forth by Deleuze. Repetition is created (generally) against a background of difficulty, and experience in the world is in some way fundamentally adverse; it has the character of a test — a test of powers (or prowess). Powers are of bodies, as Deleuze reminds us, thinking of Spinoza. Yet, as Spinoza himself asserts, we do not know what bodies can do. Depending on the situation, they may be able to create the positive reality of repetition out of the mere given of biological existence, which otherwise presses upon one as affliction or as hostile circumstance.

Work/Contingency/Knowledge

We might now examine how the poet deals with the experience of work. Poems such as "The Exposed Nest" and "Mending Wall" show once again how Frost finds it impossible to write a largely meditative poetry. He is too much aware of the practical demands of experience to be satisfied with representing a detached meditative state. Thus he prefers to write poems that dramatize the choices individuals make as they negotiate particular situations, or as they are confronted with the results of prior choices. In this sense, he retains a certain connection with classical literature, since for him, as for Aristotle, poetry represents the actions of men and women. Yet what is the context in which actions are undertaken and what is the nature of what opposes them? To what extent will the creative be forthcoming, and to what extent will mere repetitions be imposed, whether by nature or by a social context? The topic of work dramatizes these questions in a particularly clear way. It is inevitably a concrete education in tact, intelligent observation, and respect: the tact to refrain from going too far with a particular intervention (especially when it seems to be working), the intelligence to recognize the nature of the situation, and respect for the things one works with — for tools, materials, for nature, for oneself, and for others. Yet I do not want to confine myself merely to descriptions of the literal process of labor per se. Certainly we do find some of that in Frost's poetry, and such descriptions can have philosophical resonance. Nevertheless, my focus is more on the overall context that the enterprise of work creates. In essence it is a social process. In fact Frost himself says this explicitly in an early poem:

> "Men work together," I told him from the heart,
> "Whether they work together or apart."

The fact of work is not merely a physical one, and not merely individual or personal; it is fundamentally social. As Heidegger's analysis of tools and tool use suggests, there cannot really be a purely private and personal project of work (anymore than there can be a private language). The fact of meaningful labor implies a social context that has defined already, to a large degree, what would count as meaningful and productive and has provided already some of the means to pursue it, as well as the standards by which to gauge and evaluate it. In our discussion we will want especially to focus on this social dimension, because it is here that the ethical and psychological implications are most clearly revealed. In Frost's poetry, humans create themselves and their world by working; by working they establish and enact their relationship to it and to the others in it. And yet this process can produce both positive and negative results. In fact, Frost does explore some of the consequences of what we would have to call alienated labor in a number of poems, though we will not have space to examine all of these examples in detail.

Teaching and the Avowed Community

Before entering fully into his depictions of the world of labor let us try to focus part of the underlying background that tends to be implied in his depictions of working. To do this we might look at a lesser-known poem, "The Exposed Nest." It is a poem spoken to a child and so is a poem of instruction and initiation. As such it places us on the threshold of the world of work, and that liminal position might allow us to see more clearly some of the values which arise from it.

As in "Waiting," the setting is again a field, yet everything is different. In the former poem the field had been a setting for a passive observer, a person who watches, thinks, and inhales the scent of things but does nothing. The present poem differs not only in overt incident but in style as well. The verse, for instance, is brisker and has a more direct relation than any we have seen so far to the spoken idiom. In fact, since the subject involves relationships to others implied in work, one of its preoccupations will actually be tone and the speaking voice, and so it will provide one of the first opportunities for his writing to engage with the issue of tone and the dramatically situated speaking voice, one of is career-long preoccupations.

In order to establish the context it is important to recognize the role of chance in the poem, for every crucial point in the narrative has been determined by chance: by some unaccountable chance the birds have been left deserted; the cutter bar happens not to kill them; and by chance they are discovered by the speaker and his helper. We cannot miss the suggestion of a world in which the fortuitous and random are powerful determining elements, influencing events at every point. Yet clearly this is not the whole story, and in fact we find that it is balanced by large areas of predictability and order, one example of which is the seasonal recurrence that the poem tacitly acknowledges. Thus, reality is not completely random; though frequently unpredictable in detail, it is not chaotic and many of its aspects are qualitatively very clear.

THE EXPOSED NEST

You were forever finding some new play.
So when I saw you down on hands and knees
In the meadow, busy with the new-cut hay,

Trying, I thought, to set it up on end,
I went to show you how to make it stay,
If that was your idea, against the breeze,
And, if you asked me, even help pretend
To make it root again and grow afresh.
But 'twas no make-believe with you today,
Nor was the grass itself your real concern,
Though I found your hand full of wilted fern,
Steel-bright June-grass, and blackening heads of clover.
'Twas a nest full of young birds on the ground
The cutter bar had just gone champing over . . .

The first 14 lines summarize the overall intention of the piece, for there we see in synopsis its main theme of work as this is pursued against the world of nature. Yet the poem begins not with work but with play, or rather with the recollection of a time when there was only play: "You were forever finding some new play." The line succinctly characterizes a phase of childhood, which we might simply call innocence, when life and play are nearly the same thing. Yet this edenic state cannot last beyond a certain point, and it is the passing beyond this point that the poem deftly (and respectfully) portrays. Reality naturally calls the child out of self-involved play into the greater reality of the actual world. It is significant that the first line concludes with the word "play" and line ten with the word "concern." One might trace an arrow down the right-hand margin connecting the two. This developing awareness is partly a natural process and partly something learned, this latter being assisted by the adult speaker who provides a discreet and tactful guidance, not so much through any specific directions as through his general and tutelary presence. Thus, one of the insights presented is that of the delicate balance in human beings between the natural and the cultural; between nature allowing consciousness to emerge on its own, and the cultural endeavor of teaching, which the speaker provides. Yet this gradual development must be built up out of the ground of initial innocence, incorporating it and not merely displacing it (hence the speaker's gentle and respectful tone). The enthusiasms of innocence must be brought gently out into the larger world of risk without being destroyed in the process.[4]

In "The Exposed Nest," we glimpse the moment in which the awareness of the separation between the "I" of self and the "It" of the world begins to assume a new depth and importance and to acquire a moral dimension. In that initial opening outward, the otherness and uncertainty of the world are taken in and placed in counterpoint to a new-found capacity for concern and commitment. The poem therefore is one of education, and it is spoken by an adult to a child. The speaker participates in the child's growing awareness and also guides it. At the beginning, he is willing to pretend, to "play." Yet it is important to note that the speaker guides this discovery of reality through his actions, and not merely by talking. These actions bespeak an analogous participation in the life of the natural world on his part, a "taking care," in this case of a group of nestlings. We can see then that an ethic of attentiveness informs the whole poem: in attending to things, the speaker attends to the child as well by providing an example through which it concretely discovers truths about the world; as a further manifestation, this circle of attentiveness includes the small birds, and doubtless many other things as well. Yet this concern is balanced by a realistic awareness of its own limits. At some point things must be let go. This is explicit in the conclusion where they must give the birds up to chance, and implicit in this is the future act of letting go which the speaker will have to perform with the child, giving the child up to the world, to adulthood, to chance and choice. Thus, both the connectedness and the separateness of things is affirmed through the act of working. People work together, are together, and the social context is the only possible context for the meaning of their labor, and yet they are inescapably apart as well; likewise humans dwell along with nature, yet create their own order within it — culture — the essential vehicle of which is the teaching relationship itself. However, though social relations are the necessary context for human life, they remain always inescapably fragile, and are continually endangered by impulses within human beings themselves as well as by the nature of the world, which resists with its own elemental powers the orders and demarcations necessary to human culture. We find a crucial treatment of this situations in the well-known poem "Mending Wall."

The Fragile Community

"Mending Wall" is one of Frost's more elusive poems; more than any other single piece it shows the philosophical depth and richness that the subject of work — in this case quite physical work — could sometimes call forth from him. It begins as a meditation on knowledge and meaning, on the question of how and to what extent we can be said to know the world in all its strangeness and otherness. The opening line hints at some enigma in its tone and syntax: "Something there is that doesn't love a wall . . ." How different the line would be if it read: "There is something that doesn't love a wall . . ." Aside from considerations of rhythm, something essential would be lost in the tone (always a crucial consideration in Frost). Although the original's inverted syntax is not "literary" in any negative sense, it still has a somewhat ceremonial accent that enables it to give us the impression of being introduced to something rather mysterious. This could never be the case with the flat and final "There is something that . . ." The difference is between the language of propositional statement, which posits a definite matter of fact, and the language of meditation, inference, and suggestion, which weighs and considers, seeking an insight which may or may not come. In the following lines, the speaker attempts to tell us what that "something" is. Yet the most he can give us is a listing of its effects:

> [it] sends the frozen-ground-swell under it
> And spills the upper boulders in the sun,
> And makes gaps even two can pass abreast.

At this point the poet suddenly breaks off, shifting to a different subject:

> The work of hunters is another thing:
> I have come after them and made repair
> Where they have left not one stone on a stone . . .

We are told what this something is not, but not what it is or what it might be. Yet we know that it was no human agency that spilled the boulders and made the gaps. The poet returns to this question of agency and origination as though to a persistent and baffling problem:

> The gaps I mean,
> No one has seen them made or heard them made,
> But at spring mending-time we find them there.

By this point we realize that it is impossible to know, or even name, the "something" and in fact it remains so throughout the poem. The poet, interestingly, refuses to propose any metaphor or image by which it might be characterized. We may have the intuition of underlying processes which might be the cause of the various phenomena, yet everything the speaker knows about these comes at second hand, through the mediation of the wall itself and the behavior of stones. Is knowing the "something" only by mediation a disadvantage? Not really, for surface is as good as depth here in a nature where apparent and unapparent continually change. Moreover, in pragmatist fashion, we know that there is no doing that does not foster some kind of understanding. Yet here, the wall's disruption, though it recurs every year, is no less mysterious for being entirely familiar. It is familiar for being worked with and for being recurrent; and yet it is mysterious for being always hidden behind its effects. Indeed we do not know if there is a depth beneath this surface at all. But in so far as we imagine one, it must be both mysterious and familiar, known and unknown. Its effects, though, when they are more carefully considered, remain uncanny: "No one has seen them made or heard them made," we are told of these gaps, these blank spots in the constructions which humans have repeatedly erected to demarcate the otherwise unmeasured expanse of earth. This, too, is striking — that the effect, though known, seen, and in fact handled, remains troubling and elusive behind its very clarity, its being evident, and this quite apart from the entire issue of depth, which is now clearly segregated from it. It is as if the surface is revealed in its own right and in its own terms, yet for all that remains strange nonetheless. We might say that the puzzling and opaque aspects of nature force the speaker to take a pragmatic attitude toward what he can intuit yet not know. There is a reversal of the theoretical attitude, therefore, which attempts to confine itself to conceptual understanding and deliberately ignores questions of practice. Instead, the speaker is forced to limit himself to purposive action which yields limited and provisional knowledge and to turn aside from attempts at theoretical projection.

In addition, we notice that the poem is deliberately oblique in describing the wall or the effort to rebuild it. It is as if representation itself reaches a limit, and when it does, it simply stops, and the poem takes other directions, in particular, veiled and partly humorous portraiture. The piece is disjunctive, therefore, in organization, and, in addition, its mood is peculiar, alternately amusing and enigmatic, even riddling. It may border on the jocular at times but seems on the whole rather grave. For one thing, and in contrast to a long, almost immemorial tradition, spring thaw is seen as more an agent of disintegration than of revitalization; and the poem's emphasis is almost entirely on this idea of breakup, of entropic dispersal, as opposed to organic renewal or rebirth. This strikes me as a rather interesting and significant feature of the work. But in order to appreciate this we must try to get a sense of how unusual an approach this actually is. We might, for example, compare the piece to some other modern — in fact self-consciously modern — spring poems. One that suggests itself is William Carlos Williams's "By the road to the contagious hospital . . . " Here we find a deliberate attempt to infuse this genre with new vigor.

> By the road to the contagious hospital
> under the surge of the blue
> mottled clouds driven from the

northeast — a cold wind. Beyond, the
waste of broad, muddy fields
brown with dried weeds, standing and fallen

patches of standing water
the scattering of tall trees

All long the road the reddish
purplish, forked, upstanding, twiggy
stuff of bushes and small trees
with dead, brown leaves under them
leafless vines —

Lifeless in appearance, sluggish
dazed spring approaches —

They enter the new world naked,
cold, uncertain of all save
that they enter. All about them
the cold, familiar wind —

Now the grass, tomorrow —
the stiff curl of wildcarrot leaf
One by one objects are defined —
It quickens: clarity, outline of leaf

But now the stark dignity of
entrance — Still, the profound change
has come upon them: rooted, they
grip down and begin to awaken

Here spring is "Lifeless in appearance," and "sluggish"; and one's attention is directed to "muddy fields / brown with dried weeds" and "patches of standing water." Yet Williams's poem still participates in some of the traditional motifs. There is the wind, which is cold and "familiar," completely ordinary. It is quite different from the Wordsworthian "gentle breeze"; yet it still functions as a source of energy in the piece, making the reader feel its presence and creating the sense of an active and vital reality which the poet tries to catch at its harshest and bleakest. After the wind has swept over the brownish landscape enough, and after the poet has tallied its monotony of brown leaves, muddy fields, and forked, upstanding twiggy stuff, the real subject of the poem emerges — for emergence is precisely its concern — as the gradual development of spring's particulars is carefully noted: " . . . tomorrow — / the stiff curl of wildcarrot leaf / One by one objects are defined — / It quickens: clarity, outline of leaf. . . . " At this point the tone of the description itself "quickens" as the poet begins to imagine the irruption of the full spring. Yet he checks his enthusiasm somewhat in the final stanza:

> But now the stark dignity of
> entrance — Still, the profound change
> has come upon them: rooted, they
> grip down and begin to awaken

Here the accent is more temperate and sober with a direct awareness of fact. The lyricism which had begun to quicken in the penultimate stanza was a lyricism of the later spring, and the poet, like one of his Puritan forerunners, does not want the sensuous and beguiling elaboration but the primitive and essential, the bare root and origin. He seeks to lay open to direct apprehension the naked reality of life by focusing on the very moment of its emergence, for this moment alone possesses the "stark dignity of entrance." In effect, he attempts to glimpse the point where existence originates, to focus awareness on the moment when it marks itself off from an undefined temporal ground. He attempts to do this through a kind of empirical vision based on sight itself and the unadorned naming of his decidedly plain style. For these reasons the poem is really quite traditional, and in fact is rather Wordsworthian in its own way. (Wordsworth was of course a master of evoking similar scenes of drab cold bleakness.) Despite the absence of transcendental intuitions, the basic impulse is analogous — to intuit an inner truth of nature by direct visual perception.

Frost, however, excludes all of this, just as he refuses to name the "something." By comparison his poem seems to lack direction, meandering from point to point in a rather devious way and, as I have already mentioned, containing a number of oddly disjunctive rhetorical moves. There is the slight drift from the announced subject at line five ("The work of hunters is another thing . . . ") and the sudden return to it four lines later ("The gaps I mean . . . "); a sudden half-facetious exclamation ("Stay where you are until our backs are turned . . . "); or the sudden odd dismissal of the whole project ("Oh, just another kind of outdoor game, / One on a side. It comes to little more . . . "). It is as if the poem's rhetorical strategies were as much in danger of fragmenting as the wall itself, and in many ways the poem is more daring in this very disjunctiveness than the Williams piece, despite its being written in blank verse and complete sentences. The speaker's thoughts move about from one aspect of the situation to another, at one moment describing his immediate activity, at another making generalizations about it, at other times jokes, and at still others contemplative and serious *sententiae*. In the course of all this, the reader comes to understand such shifting about as part of a deliberate strategy to accommodate experience. For in each of the attitudes mentioned a different approach to the situation is attempted and then set aside. And though one might feel at moments that the poem is too self-consciously a heuristic exercise designed to tease the reader, there is a definite gravity about it; it moves with a deliberateness that bespeaks a genuine and deep involvement with some fundamental problem. It has, for instance, a slowness of pace that is in strong contrast to any other spring poem I can think of: the poem, quite simply, plods. Such a deliberate pace seems to indicate an attempt to deal with a disruption that threatens to become complete disintegration. One comes to suspect that its underlying occasion is a recognition of the problem of entropy, and that its purpose is to test ways of adjusting to this.

Yet this very pragmatism poses its own danger, that of a complacence before the fundamental mystery. In order to avoid this mistake, the speaker must be reminded not only of the mystery of the natural world itself, but also of the superficiality of his understanding of it and the fragility of his means of dealing with it (however effective they may be in many cases). Yet it is clear that the speaker does not merely act but also meditates. In fact his action and meditation are intimately connected, if not one, so that there is an overcoming of the dualism implicit in the narrative. One attains insight by handling things, and likewise by handling one's neighbor. Yet there must at some point be an extrapolation from the purely pragmatic realm to some more theoretical formulation based upon that. There seems to be a definite reluctance to take this step. Yet both the stones one handles and the neighbor one speaks to are dealt with against a larger background, and this inevitably suggests broader concerns and more broadly significant generalizations than the piece has allowed itself so far.

We have already noted how spring is represented in a rather unusual way: in place of the traditional theme of renewal, we are presented with a vision of disruption. In fact, we find the strange statement (on the part of the protagonist); "Spring is the mischief in me," he tells us, and he goes on to question the need of having walls at all, a need which his neighbor, who knows only what he has been told, naturally assumes. What sort of mischief is this? Surely the poet is aligning himself with the forces of disorder. If this is the case, then his riddling comments can be seen as a minor version of the spirit of revolutionary outbreak which, in Romantic literature, is sometimes associated with spring and which is seen as the human manifestation of that welling up of vital energy which we intuit in the natural world. In an American context the overtly political significance of this theme is frequently muted. Yet in *Walden*, for example, Thoreau sees the spring as bringing an apocalyptic transfiguration of nature. His thawing hillside which resembles human organs is an image of nature turned inside out by the forces which are latent in it and which can rise to heights of vision in the man who, completely renewed, sees the sun as but a morning star. There may be a similar vision of renewal in Frost's poem, but if so it is expressed without a sense of a necessary and radical historical break, but rather in terms that suggest a less spectacular, more mundane process of change. Indeed the depths of nature, the depths beneath the ground, are deliberately ignored in favor of surface events that yet are seen as having implications beyond their immediate context, rippling outward through the social world. Perhaps there is the suggestion that we should find some way of configuring this world so that productive effects would be conserved and amplified and destructive ones dissipated. There is no sense that Frost has any idea of foregoing things like property and its supposed rights, yet perhaps we are to understand that our society might be made more amenable to the powers of renewal and innovation which the narrator feels burgeoning around him and welling up within. Perhaps he even senses them in his brute neighbor whom, significantly, unlike Thoreau, he does not actually call by that name, but whose hidebound and robotic conservatism he ascribes to his father and, no doubt, by implication, to a long line of fathers.

Therefore, implicit in such an access of vital force, which yet is present only in a very mediated and indirect way, is the idea of a revised social order. Renewed men will require a society similarly renewed, and the old ways must go. The mischief in him is the recognition of the arbitrary nature of social forms, and, at a deeper level, of the conventionality of form itself, of demarcation, definition, though not, significantly, limit as such, which is something that nothing can exist without. With the coming of spring, however, a new and primitive energy makes itself felt, not in overt or dramatic ways, indeed in very insinuating, indirect ways about as conspicuous as a given boulder or group of boulders being slightly out of alignment. Subtle changes, internal to the speaker and dimly sensed around him, and then seen in small but somewhat more clear and determinate ways, make the poet aware of the tempting fragility of all social and cultural constructs, of all things which mark, divide, measure or orient, and he cannot help but grow impatient with them. His momentary impulse is to do away with all. And yet this is only momentary, for the spectacle of his brute neighbor, who is both helper and antagonist, and who at one point, perhaps alarmingly, wields two large rocks, makes one realize that there might indeed be some obscure threat of violence here. We cannot say what will happen or might happen between these two, yet certainly such tonal ambiguities in the piece as we have already mentioned require this word of qualification serving to reconfirm a sense of the necessity of walls and other structures, for we can not overlook the minatory suggestion of "I see him there, / Bringing a stone grasped firmly by the top / In each hand, like an old-stone savage armed." The wall, therefore, does serve as a marker and so makes the lay of things more comprehensible. Perhaps the only real mistake is to regard it in an unquestioning manner, as the neighbor apparently does. From this standpoint, insight consists in taking achieved forms seriously, but not, as it were, literally; there is no sense in which they are as real as the natural forces upon which they are built, and of which they are in a sense manifestations. Yet it is wise to see their pragmatic value in ordering and separating, in bringing definition, however disputable, and clarity, however contestable.

"Two things continually threaten the world: order and disorder," Valéry tells us. It is into such a dialectic that the poem resolves. We might assign the role of Order to our brute neighbor, for he seems to function as the representative of every conservative impulse by which individuality is sacrificed to some collective wisdom designed to keep things as they are. He is an example of that primitive human stubbornness which holds tenaciously to what has always been done because it is familiar and works. Against such an Order nature itself militates through the agency of spring. It is an unhappy story, given the crudity of the forces pitted against each other. Yet in our experience we often do find this to be the case — an oppressive, constricting order and an anarchic disorder each contending for its share of our life. In such a context (or contest) the poet is the man in the middle, mediating between these contraries and attempting to balance them against each other. The speaker works to shore up the wall against spring's disruptions, but at the same time he questions the wisdom of having walls and attempts to "put a notion" in his neighbor's head. The notion does not stick, of course, and the poet even lets his dense interlocutor have the last word: "Good fences make good neighbors." Again we see Frost's distance from Romantic rhetoric: he refuses to imagine an alternative social order or the abolition of social demarcations. Mine/Yours; Us/Them; the inescapable drudgery of life; the obscure and inhospitable physical world; the liability of things to decay; the fragility of order; the barely suppressed hostility of one's neighbor — all these are considered in the poem and managed through the process of physical labor itself. Though it forces one to deal with the resistant and enigmatic nature of the world, as well as with one's irrational or potentially dangerous collaborator, such work is also revealed as an essential power which keeps the speaker from being reduced to a merely physical being or to a merely social being — both states exemplified by the brute neighbor. The positive and the creative are developed out of resistance, and contingent order out of shifting and enigmatic events. The careful, circumspect dealing which brings this about in practical affairs, and which the poem portrays, is matched on an intellectual plane by a nuanced and in some ways self-effacing style which attempts to track the event — whether it be an occurrence in the natural world or someone's speech and behavior — with a combination of alertness and restraint and which will not attempt to impose too much form or too much style while yet maintaining some form and some style. In this way an otherness is allowed into the poetry, the otherness of events and also of persons.

The Voice of the Other

And yet what is this merely social being to which one's neighbor has been reduced? René Char says that the poet's task is to number the faces of the living. In his narrative pieces Frost attempts this. As a recorder of character, he allows the living faces of these others to be present, inscribed in the elegance of his language, like the dim forms glimpsed in the sand at the bottom of the stream. They are often the most marginal of people and yet they are seen and preserved in the limpid fluency of his verse. Certainly there is a visuality present in these pieces, as in all his work: one thinks of the deft descriptions of the empty farmhouse in "The Black Cottage" or the imagistic touches in "The Fear" which convey a sense of the surrounding darkness and isolation. And yet I believe he approached this part of his work, an ethical task of responsiveness to others, perhaps more by means of the ear than of the eye. These very poems indicate this: the voice of the narrator in "The Black Cottage," concerned, educated, somewhat condescending with respect to the life of the old woman which he recounts, yet ultimately grieved; and in the second, the fearful and yet subtly manipulative tones of the wife, and the puzzled, small, helpless bravado of her new husband.

In this type of writing, the poet becomes a witness to human speech, and his task is to open his language itself, the thing which is closest to him, to the spontaneous and unforeseeable, to these aural signatures his fellow men and women create daily, hourly, in their language as it is manifest in their spoken words. It is a practice which disproves Bakhtin's strange assertions that the dialogic imagination is the exclusive province of novels and can never be present in poetry. In these poems we see that it is, or rather we hear it. Yet to accomplish this, the poet must be capable of an almost Deleuzian feeling for the unchartable "flows" to which he must open his learned and acquired discipline of prosody. Frost's various remarks about sentence sounds make one imagine that he perceived crucial aspects of human existence — in particular the realities of affliction and oppression — through his imagination of voice, however much his botanist's eye was drawn by visual detail. Thus, rather than the Levinasian face, it is the voice as captured in a deliberately flexible and inclusive style which becomes the vehicle for recognizing otherness. In the process, we hear, among many other things certainly, the tones of violation as these reach us from the very margins of the social sphere and not infrequently the voice of incipient mental breakdown. In this we are made to recognize the fragility of the human before its own repressive and exclusive social structures, and before its own inherent violence.

We recall in this connection that in *Erotism, The Accursed Share*, and other works, Georges Bataille develops a speculative anthropology in which work — the necessity for humans to work, and the overall world of work which this creates and on which any functional economy depends — is set off against three other forces, opposite and refractory tendencies in human beings which continually threaten the orderly structures of the functional and the economic. These are, first, the erotic itself; then, a tendency toward excessive and wasteful expenditure; and finally violence — the three complexly intertwined in a dark economy of transgression. In *Erotism* in particular, Bataille contrasts the world of work with an anarchic yet always present tendency for human communities to erupt in violence — whether against strangers or against their own members.[5]

I believe that we can see these tendencies clearly illustrated in a number of Frost's narrative pieces. In the marginal rural world his narratives create we find repeatedly, placed against the background of ongoing labor characteristic of such a setting, the suggestion of violence or of the threat of violence just barely held in check by social constraints, or else we find the representation of violence actually committed or its aftermath. Certainly it is not possible here to give an extended account of this body of work, a substantial portion of his total output which has nonetheless never been fully done justice to (this book being no exception on that score). In this type of writing, as in drama, a genre Frost aspired to, the attunement of the author to the resonance and waywardness of voice enables the underlying psychological and moral dimension of human beings in their social existence to appear with special clarity. When it does, we are made to realize that this social existence is often quite negative and is frequently constrained and distorted by the very fact of work itself, which takes the form of exploited labor, impoverishment and drudgery, or else, in an opposite circumstance, that it is marred by eruptions of violation, insult, and indeed murder, whether premeditated and rationalized in some way or blatantly irrational and spontaneous.

"A Servant to Servants"

This poem is often viewed as a portrait of someone succumbing to schizophrenia. The speaker is overwhelmed by the sheer volume of physical work she is expected to do — a situation not unfamiliar to any number of women at her time or indeed even our own, and so there is a continual pressure on her, a pressure not merely of the kind we are habitually disposed to think of in connection with the world of work — one of time deadlines, financial considerations, and the like — but a more brute and existentially pressing matter of numbers of men, numbers of dishes, of meals, and so forth. The volume of work changes it into something different: into a means by which an individual's very personality is buried under the sheer quantity of things to be attended to and the physical labor required in this. The frayed, desperate, and needy aspects of the speaker's personality come forth strongly and are particularly clear indications of exactly this type of dehumanization, for that in essence is what it is:

> Bless you, of course you're keeping me from work,
> But the thing of it is, I need to *be* kept.
> There's work enough to do — there's always that;
> But behind's behind. The worst that you can do
> Is set me back a little more behind.
> I shan't catch up in this world, anyway.
> I'd *rather* you'd not go unless you must.

We should read the first line, I think, as a response to a question: "Are we keeping you?" There would be a heavy accent, most likely, on the word "course." Read in this way, and with the succeeding lines, we hear the suggestion of a voice attempting humor at its own situation but at the same time willing to confess its trouble and even desperation. It is a veiled way of asking for assistance, or if not that at least for recognition.

Yet it would have to be a type of recognition that would exceed the realm of mere politeness and would involve awareness on the visitors' part of the full extent of misery, estrangement, and isolation which are conveyed elsewhere in her account. Sentimentality and self-pity are avoided by means of this humor and by a certain deliberate casualness that Frost's grasp of the "folksy" idiom of the time is well able to convey. But the isolation and desperation remain and are conveyed in the last line. She asks others to stay, to not go unless they must, and so we also glimpse a loneliness which is itself part of this very exploitation: she is dealt with in an almost anonymous mode, as a machine would be (though the seasonally hired farm hands are themselves exploited as well). Human-to-human interaction defined as the free and un-coerced interchange of entire personalities with their desires, dreams, and thoughts is a type of experience which she is almost entirely denied. Hence her desperation: she seems almost to be holding onto the coat sleeves of her visitors at the end of the poem, imploring them not to go unless they must. There is thus, in a way not accounted for in Bataille's analysis (though it is certainly in Marx's), a violence inherent in work itself, and yet this work, though dehumanizing, perhaps keeps at bay a greater or more explicit violence — that of the men, to say nothing of her husband and the sexual demands he makes upon her. This erotic dimension, in fact, is presented in a rather lurid and grotesque episode:

> My father's brother, he went mad quite young.
> Some thought he had been bitten by a dog,
> Because his violence took on the form
> Of carrying his pillow in his teeth;
> But it's more likely he was crossed in love,
> Or so the story goes. It was some girl.
> Anyway all he talked about was love.
> They soon saw he would do someone a mischief
> If he wa'n't kept strict watch of, and it ended
> In father's building him a sort of cage,
> Or room within a room, of hickory poles,
> Like stanchions in the barn, from floor to ceiling —
> A narrow passage all the way around.
> Anything they put in for furniture
> He'd tear to pieces, even a bed to lie on.
> So they made the place comfortable with straw,
> Like a beast's stall, to ease their consciences.
> Of course they had to feed him without dishes.
> They tried to keep him clothed, but he paraded

With his clothes on his arm — all of his clothes.
Cruel — it sounds. I s'pose they did the best
They knew. And just when he was at the height,
Father and mother married, and mother came,
A bride, to help take care of such a creature,
And accommodate her young life to his.
That was what marrying father meant to her.
She had to lie and hear love things made dreadful
By his shouts in the night.

There are, therefore, sketched out in the poem, two orders of violence, the one more explicit, the other more suggested: the first is the immediate order of work and its obvious dehumanization; the second is the order of sexual exploitation, and perhaps perversion, which the poem is much more vague about, but which is present not so much as a factor in the speaker's literal experience, but as a potential she cannot help but be aware of and which no doubt colors her perception of the hired men who lodge with her in the same house and whom she must wait on.

We have four here to board, great good-for-nothings,
Sprawling about the kitchen with their talk
While I fry their bacon. Much they care!
No more put out in what they do or say
Than if I wasn't in the room at all.
Coming and going all the time, they are:
I don't learn what their names are, let alone
Their characters, or whether they are safe
To have inside the house with doors unlocked.
I'm not afraid of them, though, if they're not
Afraid of me.

The routine of work keeps the more dire possibilities at bay to some extent. And yet, the overall picture we are given is of violence and violation, if only in the form of a gradual attrition — physical and mental. In this particular poem at least, neither work nor Eros has anything redeeming in it, but both are manifest as powers of degradation; the self which must deal with both is caught in a continual position of affliction and oppression. The technical accomplishment is to allow this to be heard using iambic pentameter. It is a dramatic achievement, fundamentally, for it consists of opening the verse itself to the demands of self-presentation on the part of a speaker. In this instance it is a self-presentation which is both forthright and guarded, and the writing conveys this peculiar tone consisting of humor, small narrow hopes, and fears based upon past trauma. We have moved to an almost opposite pole in relation to some of the poems with which I began this study. Here there seems to be almost no possibility of making work, effort against resistance, or the repetition involved, into constructive powers. They are merely things to be endured. And yet the author's account of the world of labor and effort, resistance and opposition, the general encounter of the human with its genuine otherness, would not be complete without attention paid to the shadow realms to which this all too often does lead. There are, however, perhaps even darker regions than what we find presented in this piece.

"The Vanishing Red"

In this neglected and, in fact, rather strange poem, racist violence is directed against a native American man, someone who clearly is excluded from the society and overall economy of the white world on whose fringes he exists. He is made the victim of a spontaneous and irrational irruption of violence, which, interestingly, happens at the site of a mill, a place of work in itself and beyond that a place that can be taken as symbolic of the overall economy which supports the community in question, but from which he is excluded.

> He is said to have been the last Red Man
> In Acton. And the Miller is said to have laughed—
> If you like to call such a sound a laugh.
> But he gave no one else a laugher's license.
> For he turned suddenly grave as if to say,
> "Whose business — if I take it on myself,
> Whose business — but why talk round the barn? —
> When it's just that I hold with getting a thing done with."
>
> You can't get back and see it as he saw it.
> It's too long a story to go into now.
> You'd have to have been there and lived it.
> Then you wouldn't have looked on it as just a matter
> Of who began it between the two races.

The poem in its objectivity does not attempt to judge the miller's action. Yet this should not cause us to misunderstand the meaning of the second stanza. We are told in effect that the situation in its existential complexity is historically irrecoverable: we would have to *be* the miller in order to see the situation as he did. The poem makes no attempt to explain how he did in fact see it or why a mere sound should set him off in this way. This is allowed to remain inexplicable. Yet the poem does make clear that the violence in question is an impulsive force, one tied to the concrete and embodied existence of the individual in question, indeed of both individuals. This is why the essence of the situation cannot be recovered, and why abstract explanations of an historical and sociological nature, though valid in their way, must always omit the crucial factors unique to the particular individuals who act and suffer. The broad historical forces are always instantiated in actual persons, who inevitably are lost to cultural memory, at least in part. Thus though the incident certainly *is* a matter of "who began it between the races," it cannot be *just* that because no incident could be. It would be relatively easy to write a poem condemning such an action. But Frost takes on the more difficult task of enabling us to glimpse the impulsive and irrational core that all such actions must have. The work does not present us with the voice of the Other, as "A Servant to Servants" does, nor does the individual in question — "the last Red Man" — really appear in it. On the contrary, it is a kind of trap door down which he disappears. Instead, in presenting a violent incident in some of its detail, it contributes to a "thick description" of the forces active in a given social context in a particular place and time.

The violence itself is interesting not only in its off-hand manner but also in the visceral occasion which prompts it — a particular sound which the "Red Man" happened to make, one that, for some reason physically disgusts the miller to such an extent that he commits the atrocity in question. Again this seems to me to point out that social and political relations are never understandable in only abstract and theoretical terms, since they involve actual people — creatures who are physical, more governed by passion than by reason, and sometimes opaque to themselves, possessed by impulses they do not understand. Here, in fact, the Red Man's spontaneous expression of his own temperament and experience — the sound he makes — is subject to a complete rejection, one that extends to the rest of his existence, in fact. What exactly was it, one wonders. An expression of surprise at what? The poem is silent about this. The victim's subjectivity is not allowed to be present in the work at all, just as, analogously, and on a broader scale, it was not allowed to be in the society of the time, nor, to a large extant, in the cultural and historical record. It is a brutal poem certainly, and yet quite realistic in its representation of the nature of irrational violence, a violence which does not need a substantive reason for its occasion and which does not need a substantive rationale for its pseudo-justification. The physical reality of the Other is enough, and some immediate subrational sense of the difference between that Other and oneself.

Conclusion

The movement outward into alterity which we have seen in Frost's style and which we have attempted to characterize takes the form of a searching for the creatively singular in the context of oppositional forces in nature and in society which would limit the individual to the realm of mere repetition or even seek to reduce him or her entirely to the subhuman. This search is driven by a desire for the real resident in everyone, a desire which yet must be fostered by positive interactions between individuals. The most significant type of interaction, from the cultural standpoint, is teaching. Teaching and desire discover the natural world and construct the human one simultaneously. Yet the negative that is encountered is not limited to the resistance and obscurity of nature. There is the oppression inherent in sociality and a violence smoldering beneath its surface, a violence that would seem to be inherent in the human person along with his or her erotic cravings, with which it is closely entangled. There is added, therefore, to the developing perception of the fragility of nature a parallel perception of the fragility of the human, both in terms of the individual, but also in terms of the collective, which is continually threatened by violent outbursts, not merely against the stranger but against its own members too. The poetry as a whole, therefore, attempts to take account of the total range of human experience, from the most idyllic to the most negative and destructive, and gives perhaps a particular emphasis to those which lie in between and which require and foster the fundamental act of learning, the process by which the foreign is encountered and dealt with. In order to do this, however, subtle but profound adjustments of style and imagination are needed which open the resources of poetry to the enigmas of nature and to all ranges of social interaction.

Part Two: Person, Place, and World

Introduction to Part Two

In Part Two we will turn our attention to a range of thematic considerations that will enable us to fill in the picture of Frost's poetic universe that we are attempting to create. Certainly there were thematic considerations in Part One as well, but there our objective was focused more on illustrating the main courses of its stylistic change from its early phase to its maturity. In addition, we tried to suggest the reasons why this type of change, and these types of stylistic traits, were necessary. Our focus was in some respects, therefore, in the realm of "poetics" broadly considered. Yet it was a poetics based upon a certain conception of reality. In the remainder we will need to fill in that conception of reality a bit more. Yet we must also try to understand the author's vision of the nature of the human person which encounters that reality. We must ask, then, if he develops likewise a vision of the place where this encounter occurs and then of the world as a whole — the ultimate object of any individual's ethical concern, intellectual inquiry, or imaginative grasp.

Chapter Three begins, therefore, with an attempt to describe the nature of this individual self-hood, taking it in what we might think of as its purest and most basic forms — the relationship of the individual to his or her own passions and sensations, as these are discovered in the context of the erotic life, first, and, second, in the context of mortality or being-toward-death. These two fundamental experiences — love and the realization of mortality — cause us to discover the reality of our life and its basic passions and energies, in effect revealing the self in its purest and most basic form. As in previous chapters, we see that discovery is prompted by the encounter with alterity. Here it is the intimate alterity of the erotic as a type of experience which is at first strange and uncanny, and it is also the equally intimate alterity of death itself, which is by definition alien and yet implied in the nature of one's very physical life and experience. A curious paradox emerges from this — that those experiences which challenge the self, threaten to disorient or disrupt it, are also those which in a strange way confirm it by revealing its concrete experience to it in greatest intensity and depth. For if it is not the case that self-hood takes the form of a substantial and stable entity, neither is it the case that it is a mere illusion or conceptual mistake. It is consubstantial with the world itself and is revealed in its concrete nature as a process of perception and a responsiveness to the world and to itself.

And yet this perception and responsiveness, as it occurs always in a body, occurs likewise always in a place. Where are we in human life? In Chapter Four, we attempt to consider further the nature of the interaction between self and world as this is dramatized through the encounter between individuals and places. We take landscape as the central topic in this chapter and use it as a way of focusing the poet's further investigation of alterity, his ongoing effort to uncover deeper aspects of experience than are ordinarily dealt with or recognized, either in day-to-day life or in most writing, by placing his protagonists in a range of isolated and sometimes dangerous places. It is as if here the existential drama of human existence is allowed to unfold with a particular clarity. The nature of this drama reveals itself in the form of a quest for certainty; it is an epistemological drama in which the human agent encounters the lack of clear demarcation in nature and the uncertainty of its own perceptions, judgments, and constructions. Certainly there is an ability to create such constructions in the first place, whether they be physical or mental. Yet the overall context in which this is done is one which does not ultimately support them, or which does so only to limited extents, limits which, moreover, cannot be foreseen in advance.

To some extent these themes had already been broached in Chapter Two with the poem "Mending Wall." Now, though, they are met by the protagonist with a new note of extremity and in the context of a solitude that allows their implications to resonate all the more: with others absent and without the entire range of mediations between the self and the otherness of the world which the social context provides — mediations which are provisional but nonetheless effective — the human agent must recognize the nakedness of its situation and its fundamental exposure to the world. If the constructions of sociality and culture are not finally able to provide support and certainty, then we find ourselves moving, with surprising rapidity perhaps, into a strange world of thought and feeling, one in which the human comes to be seen as more and more accidental to the world.

Yet the degree to which human beings can actually inhabit such a thought-context is perhaps questionable. Indeed some of the psychological consequences of this situation are examined in the final section of Chapter Four, a section dealing with what we call "radical loneliness," the complete isolation of the individual in a selfhood which seems all the more isolated given its condition of being stripped not only of all certainties but also of all effective means of establishing connections and continuities between itself and its surroundings, itself and other selves. Such a circumstance creates, finally, a question about the value of human life itself — a question which arises in the reader's mind perhaps but which seems to be lurking in the author's as he moves his protagonists further into these dark and austere regions. Yet the author's ongoing receptivity to beauty — in particular to the beauty of nature — remains a factor which holds out something continually positive in human existence, despite its tragic dimension.

Accordingly, in Chapter Five we consider the poetry's final aspect, the final phase of its overall project of creating a comprehensive vision of human existence in the modern world. Here the topic is totality, or rather the attempt to imagine the life of the world as a whole. With this attempt goes naturally the attempt to imagine the ultimate relationship of humans in particular to this whole. The initial relationship, significantly, is provided by means of the eye: the human being is that which sees and witnesses the world and at the same time recognizes itself as being in some way apart from this world. This seems to be the burden of the charming poem "The Last Mowing." In the more famous "Design" we encounter a type of "thought experiment" in imagining the world without humans, and we begin to see some of the psychological implications of doing so. Here Frost shows himself as having been ahead of his time in a way that we have been in a position to appreciate only recently, since he must have been one of the first American writers to take up the theme of a post-anthropocentric world view. Yet he also shows that adopting such a view is not easy, either from an imaginative or emotional standpoint. The imaginative difficulties require the strange thought experiment of this poem, and its emotional power — often described with words such as "chilling" and the like — is an indicator of the emotional resistance we tend naturally to have to any attempt to remove the human from a place of central importance in the world. This emotional resistance is further represented in the poem "The Census Taker" where it is given voice quite explicitly as a fear of human extinction. The poet dramatizes the natural resistance we have to imagining ourselves out of the picture, and he gives voice to it in the first person: only by candidly meeting such anxieties is it possible to develop a post-anthropocentric view of the world that will be mature and in some ways acceptable and sustainable.

CHAPTER THREE

Person: Ekstasis and the Management of the Excess

Frost presents us with a vision of selfhood as a process that is realized by acting against the resistance of the physical world and in the context of complex social circumstances. And yet self-hood always exceeds itself; it is always in process and fundamentally dynamic. From this arises the poetry of subjectivity per se, the poetry of love and of the fated subjectivity that knows itself death-bound. Eros and death are the mothers of both ecstasy and beauty. To plumb the nature of the embodied self in its most fundamental moments we need at last only these two themes, and therefore two poems likewise will serve, though they are in fact two of the greatest ever written in English on their respective themes, desire and death. Yet it seems to me that these two themes, in the way they are handled here, generate a third: the desire for an ultimate contact with the reality of the world which then leads to a vehement desire for death, a desire which yet has nothing morbid about it but is envisioned as the ultimate consummation of life.

Clearly, then, these are extraordinary themes, extraordinary movements of the soul. The emotions generated must likewise be turbulent and profound. Yet here they are expressed in the poet's typical style, which, though retaining many Romantic and Pre-Raphaelite characteristics, is yet strongly oriented toward realistic detail and direct statement. How can one make such a style an idiom of ecstatic intensity? The answer, it turns out, is through the traditional devices of rhythm, meter, and sound — a sheer virtuosity of rhythm and rhyme serves him where dream-influenced image associations might serve the Surrealist, and where a deliberately artificial language might serve others such as Crane or Pound. Meter and rhyme, of all things, become the means of "making strange," of creating an idiom of transport and excess. Therefore, though it is often thought that Frost's poetry exhibits a certain limitation in tonal range, we see that it sometimes does convey moments of *ekstasis.* And yet, though it is extremely original in the way it handles such material, the substance of what it depicts is not entirely without precedent:

> Crossing a bare common, in snow puddles, at twilight, under a clouded sky, without having in my thoughts any occurrence of special good fortune, I have enjoyed a perfect exhilaration I am glad to the brink of fear. In the woods, too, a man casts off his years, as the snake his slough, and at what period soever of life, is always a child. In the woods is perpetual youth. Within these plantations of God, a decorum and sanctity reign, a perennial festival is dressed, and the guest sees not how he should tire of them in a thousand years. In the woods, we return to reason and faith. There I feel that nothing can befall me in life, — no disgrace, no calamity, (leaving me my eyes), which nature cannot repair. Standing on the bare ground, — my head bathed by the blithe air and uplifted into infinite space, — all mean egotism vanishes. I become a transparent eyeball; I am nothing; I see all; the currents of the Universal Being circulate through me; I am part or parcel of God. (Emerson, "Nature" 10)

It is a moment of vision and of what once would have been called enthusiasm. Yet the seer will not omit the bare common, the clouded sky, or the snow puddles he splashes through. In fact he seems to make them, along with the air itself, the virtual occasion for his "exhilaration." Even the strange interruption in the middle of the passage is telling: while claiming that nature will never betray this heart which loves her, that there will be "no disgrace, no calamity . . . which nature cannot repair," he yet makes the qualification "leaving me my eyes." All calamities except literal blindness can be compensated for. But the loss of sight could have no compensation. Of all the senses, sight is the most precise. Thus, we might see Emerson's insistence upon it as another indication of his concern with the factuality of the world. Rather than Plato's eye of the mind whose internalized gaze beholds a form or idea, Emerson desires the eyes in his head to be definitively opened. To this end the energy of his being flows out to meet the actual world in an access of perception so intense that, for the moment, he is "all eye." In such a passage, the particulars are not emphasized, yet the faculty by which the particulars are discovered — vision — is exalted nearly to the point of apotheosis.[1]

What is desired is surely nothing other than the revelation of the actual itself: a vision of the concrete so unmediated and ecstatic that it forces all else out of consciousness, which for the moment is occupied exclusively by vision and visibility. In its rhetorical pressures and in its momentary submersion of the self in a transfiguring experience, the passage suggests an enthusiastic impulse which has been secularized to accommodate the actual world in its mere factuality. It seeks to discover this world, to lay it bare in an unmediated vision. And it makes us perhaps reflect upon the motivation: why is this needed in the first place?

Perhaps we must be *made* to feel the reality of the world as such. There is something impossible about experience perhaps. Is this not part of the meaning of Ashbery's poetry, which often seems to be about the impossibility of truly experiencing anything? No matter what happens, there is a sense in which experience slips by us. It is a strange problem, and one Emerson was quite familiar with. In "Experience," for example, he observes:

> People grieve and bemoan themselves, but it is not half so bad with them as they say. There are moods in which we court suffering, in the hope that here at least we shall find reality, sharp peaks and edges of truth. But it turns out to be scene-painting and counterfeit. The only thing grief has taught me is to know how shallow it is. That, like all the rest, plays about the surface, and never introduces me into the reality, for contact with which we would even pay the costly price of sons and lovers. Was it Boscovich who found out that bodies never come in contact? Well, souls never touch their objects. An innavigable sea washes with silent waves between us and the things we aim at and converse with. Grief too will make us idealists. In the death of my son, now more than two years ago, I seem to have lost a beautiful estate, — no more. I cannot get it nearer to me. If tomorrow I should be informed of the bankruptcy of my principal debtors, the loss of my property would be a great inconvenience to me, perhaps, for many years; but it would leave me as it found me, — neither better nor worse. So is it with this calamity: it does not touch me: something which I fancied was a part of me, which could not be torn away without tearing me, nor enlarged without enriching me, falls off from me, and leaves no scar. It was caducous. I grieve that grief can teach me nothing, nor carry me one step into real nature. The Indian who was laid under a curse that the wind should not blow on him, nor water flow to him, nor fire burn him, is a type of us all. (Emerson 473)

Following Hartman's analysis of the function of "enthusiasm" in Smart (a poet for whom Frost is known to have had a special fondness, interestingly), we might say that enthusiasm is secularized in American literature, not necessarily to reveal what is transcendent, but simply to reveal what is. In the process, one receives not metaphysical insight, but access to the world as it is. The sense of confirmation experienced is not that things are all right, but that things are. Enthusiasm becomes a means for overcoming the estrangement between self and world, or for attempting to. There is, of course, no guarantee that such estrangement can be overcome. Yet the moment of enthusiasm is an important means for attempting to assert some connection between self and world. Since it is of short duration, it provides an important complement to the more continuous effort of engagement that work is. And yet as it takes one out of oneself, it also reveals the fragility of that self. It leads to the idea of death as the ultimate limit of self-exceeding, and it attempts to affirm this idea too in a type of *amor fati*.[2]

"To Earthward"

Among Frost's poems, "To Earthward" is characterized by an unusual lyric intensity: a passionate swirling rhythm, one of the most incantatory he ever used, and a vehement, even violent, emotion. The poem begins with a slight erotic allusion:

> Love at the lips was touch
> As sweet as I could bear;
> And once that seemed too much;
> I lived on air
>
> That crossed me from sweet things,
> The flow of — was it musk
> From hidden grapevine springs
> Downhill at dusk?
>
> I had the swirl and ache
> From sprays of honeysuckle
> That when they're gathered shake
> Dew on the knuckle.
>
> I craved strong sweets, but those
> Seemed strong when I was young;
> The petal of the rose
> It was that stung.
>
> Now no joy but lacks salt,
> That is not dashed with pain
> And weariness and fault;
> I crave the stain
>
> Of tears, the aftermark
> Of almost too much love,
> The sweet of bitter bark
> And burning clove.
>
> When stiff and sore and scarred
> I take away my hand
> From leaning on it hard
> In grass and sand,

The hurt is not enough;
I long for weight and strength
To feel the earth as rough
To all my length.

The world, after all, must come in through the mouth if life is to be sustained — one must eat, drink, breathe, and indeed conduct an erotic life of some sort. Hence Eros, which permeates one's whole being, starts as "Love at the lips." Therefore the initial impression the poem makes is not of an avid reaching toward experience, but of a shying away: a coyness and a reserve. There is humor as well, and the poet does indulge in a certain irony at the expense of his younger self: "I lived on air / That crossed me from sweet things . . . " There is a gentle mockery in the recollection of a shyness toward experience that limited itself to light tangential brushings and fleeting glimpses. We might say that the poet has lived on substitutes and that he now desires the actual, if at all possible. Certainly there is a deftly suggested comedy concerning the awkwardness of sexual awakening.

Yet there are other considerations. With the break in the middle of line six we are led into the recesses of consciousness: in that telling space, the declarative tone is broken, for the poet is overtaken by a wave of feeling which he had not experienced previously and which he did not expect. This comes in the form of a sudden memory not so different from one of Wordsworth's "spots of time," though perhaps even closer to Proust's epiphany. In Frost's case, as in Proust's, memory is unbidden and charged with the pathos of now defunct passions which, when remembered, are experienced as reminders of the ambiguous character of experience itself, its mingling of positive and negative, pleasure and pain. This sudden recollection and its puzzling, unsettling character seems to be the underlying meaning of the second stanza's concluding two-and-a-half lines with their wonderful echoing rhetorical question:

— was it musk
From hidden grapevine springs
Downhill at dusk?

The question is itself another instance of Merleau-Ponty's "being in the interrogative mood." It indicates a questioning of experience, a movement of the mind among possibilities and the movement of sense perception itself among the shifting appearances of the world in an effort to draw out from them determinate patterns and wholes. In this case, though the particulars are left vague, the sense drawn from them would seem to be the very feel of that past moment as it is recovered in at least some of its concreteness and inherent complexity, so that its specific sensuous and emotional resonance is momentarily reclaimed. Yet it would be inadequate to say that the speaker recalls this; rather he re-experiences it, relives it, albeit now very briefly. In this way the ironic mood of the opening is put aside: there is a sudden wave-like access to a deeper stratum of life. The poem is technically brilliant in the way it conveys this feeling of surprise and discovery: the sudden break catches the poet short, and catches the reader off-guard as well, and then, before either can regain their balance, throws them forward to the end of the line with its unexpected and evocative word "musk," before leading finally around the corner and through to the conclusion. The lines seem to enact an inward turning that sweeps both poet and reader into its inward spiral, plunging one into a twilit and erotically charged area of recollection.

The intensity of this early experience is acknowledged in the next stanza. Yet now we have already moved a step away from the intensity of reliving which we saw a moment ago. The tone becomes more objective, yet the description is still wonderful and the technical accomplishment no less extraordinary. "I had the swirl and ache / From sprays and honeysuckle," the poet says; and the stanza rhythmically enacts the heady excitement he speaks of. It is resolved with another surprisingly apt figure: the "dew on the knuckle" shaken out by the gathered flowers which rounds out the entire description with an image at once fresh and yet just ever so slightly, and subtly, conventional in its deft allusion to the pastoral tradition's flower gathering and the like. The purpose is perhaps to reassert a degree of control over the emotions liberated in memory by punctuating their flow with a moment of deliberate artifice. Indeed, in the next stanza it is as if the poet stands back from his recollection and assesses his former self, again with a degree of irony:

> I craved strong sweets, but those
> Seemed strong when I was young;
> The petal of the rose
> It was that stung.

We have returned to the tone of the first stanza. Yet the intervening stanzas have deepened the poet's sense of his former experience, have made him aware of its true complexity, its irreducible fusion of affirmation and negation, joy and pain. Such realization impels him to a clearer understanding of his present experience as well. The knowledge of the essential ambiguity of experience which has been gained through memory provides an insight into the nature of the present as well as to human life as such: that it is fundamentally ambiguous or paradoxical, and that it presents us with a complex of feeling both joyful and painful simultaneously:

> Now no joy but lacks salt,
> That is not dashed with pain
> And weariness and fault . . .

Perhaps there is a "fault" at the center of experience. Yet it is not a lack, it is rather temporality itself. But the poet's response is complex. He vehemently embraces experience and by extension the "fault" which he intuits within it. We recall the crucial lines:

> I crave the stain
>
> Of tears, the aftermark
> Of almost too much love,
> The sweet of bitter bark
> And burning clove.
>
> When stiff and sore and scarred
> I take away my hand
> From leaning on it hard
> In grass and sand,
>
> The hurt is not enough:
> I long for weight and strength
> To feel the earth as rough
> To all my length.

I quote the entire concluding passage because it has a musical continuity that leads the reader inevitably down the page to the final line. Yet the first thing to draw our attention is the very first line itself, broken as it is across two stanzas: the word "crave" strikes the ear as an echo — or perhaps an amplification of its use in line thirteen: "I craved strong sweets." I say amplification for it is evident that this is a different craving, something fundamentally more intense, more primitive than craving strong sweets. With a phrase such as "I crave the stain of tears . . . " we are on a different plain of experience altogether. The poet feels compelled to seize the reality of life as it is. In a sense he pushes himself outside himself, outside even the idea of pleasure or gratification of any sort. Even negative and rending experience is preferred to the feeling of not coming into full and decisive contact with the world. And at the same time he remains aware that the *suchness* of experience remains strangely elusive. The poem's very swiftness perhaps dramatizes this fact as well, that of the elusiveness of experience, while also conveying the hectic desire and heightened affect that craves contact with the world and must continue to crave, even in the face of tears, craving further and further still. No devastation resulting from a too harsh or disappointing experience is so great as that which results from the evasion of experience. The speaker can no longer afford to be so discriminating as he once was; he now craves that which is "bitter" and "burning" as well as sweet. This effort to live — for that is what the poem represents — must necessarily include the reality of suffering, and death, which the poet must affirm as much as he willed the enjoyment of pleasure.

In Frost, therefore, as in Emerson, we find enthusiastic or ecstatic states that bring selfhood beyond its typical confines, especially the narrow subjectivity that threatens to hold it in estrangement from the world. Enthusiasm is transport, but this transport must be transitive as well and point beyond itself to an object. It impels one to a desired encounter with otherness. In this sense it becomes a way of penetrating the reality of the "not me" which, as Emerson remarks, includes one's own body. The body, its total worldly context, and its past experience, all present themselves as enigmas whose nature can only be glimpsed in a state of heightened awareness.

Yet as awareness is focused on these, it must also uncover the idea of death as well, for that is inevitably implied by any and each experience if it is interrogated sufficiently and made the occasion of an exceeding of oneself. What, ultimately, does one exceed to? The poem suggests this fated mortality in its conclusion where the poet claims to "long for weight and strength / To feel the earth as rough / To all my length." This is an image that clearly fuses erotic overtones, a desire for death, and, beyond that, a desire for what we might call union with the elemental itself.[3] The contemporary American philosopher Alphonso Lingis, in explicating the phenomenology of Merleau-Ponty, identifies a progressive range of imperatives given to us directly in experience. The Kantian concept of the imperative must be expanded, he feels, or rather modified, to include direct perception. And yet perception itself is not a simple thing but a complex and ramifying phenomenon, and in fact a range of phenomena not merely *given* but rather *discoverable.* The process of discovery, it is Lingis's thesis, is not a possibility held out to a subject which chooses or declines as it pleases; rather it takes the exact form of a specific demand, an *ordinance.* The discovery of the world is not a choice but a task; and it leads one ultimately to a discovery of the elemental as such — the light in its primordial radiance, space in its boundlessness, the earth itself as inexhaustible support — and to a boundless dimension within which and according to which the elemental as such extends and endlessly exists:

> We think, then, that the world in Merleau-Ponty's sense — the light that forms a level along which color contrasts phosphoresce, the key about which the melody rises and falls, the murmur of nature from which a cry rises, the rumble of the city beneath which a moan of despair descends — these levels themselves form in a medium without dimensions or horizons — the luminosity more vast than any panorama that the light outlines in it; the vibrancy that prolongs itself outside the city and beyond the murmur of nature, the darkness more abysmal than the night from which the day dawns and into which it confides itself. We submit that the world itself is set in depths, in uncharted abysses, where there are vortices in which the body that lets loose its hold on the levels of the world . . . gets drawn. . . .
>
> But we also mean to argue that if the sensibility is drawn into these vortices beyond the nexus of levels where the world offers things, it is drawn imperatively. (Lingis, *Rereading Merleau-Ponty* 229)

Is this not a vision compatible to the one we find in the intense final stanza of Frost's poem? Do we not find there an elemental imperative to fuse one's being with the earthly itself? And yet we find what is perhaps the prefiguration of both in the following passage from Emerson's "Circles" :

> The one thing which we seek with insatiable desire is to forget ourselves, to be surprised out of our propriety, to lose our sempiternal memory and to do something without knowing how or why; in short to draw a new circle. Nothing great was ever achieved without enthusiasm. The way of life is wonderful, it is by abandonment. (Emerson 178)

It is such an "abandonment" which Frost seeks in "To Earthward" and which Lingis finds as well in his own, different way. To this end, the poet wishes to cast off the burden of the self and its habitual mechanisms of defense, which are seen as a major impediment to such an ultimate encounter. We might even observe in the concluding stanzas, a marked intensity that suggests a forceful and even fierce determination:

> When stiff and sore and scarred
> I take away my hand
> From leaning on it hard
> In grass and sand,
>
> The hurt is not enough:
> I long for weight and strength
> To feel the earth as rough
> To all my length.

By this point the poem has gained momentum and quickened to a more overtly passionate speech; indeed there is a note of vehemence, almost of violence, which is resolved in the last lines, not in calm or acceptance, but with a kind of resolute seizing of mortality. The poem thus exhibits the manifestations of a powerful and even willful subjectivity that indeed has its almost savage side. This contrasts with most of what we find in Emerson, who can be sober or even grim, as he is in "Experience," yet who is never fierce. The conclusion of "Circles" quoted above seems almost genial in comparison to Frost's poem. A closer parallel might be found in Thoreau, at the powerful climax of his Ktaadn episode:

> I stand in awe of my body, this matter to which I am bound has become so strange to me. I fear not spirits, ghosts, of which I am one, — that my body might, — but I fear bodies, I tremble to meet them. What is this Titan that has possession of me? Talk of mysteries! — Think of our life in nature, — daily to be shown matter, to come in contact with it, — rocks, trees, wind on our cheeks! The *solid* earth! The *actual* world! The *common sense! Contact! Contact! Who are we? where are we?* (*Maine Woods* 71)

This view of the body as "other" does derive from Emerson. Yet in Emerson we find nothing like Thoreau's awareness of its potentially horrifying aspect. At the same time it is clear that Thoreau desires an immediate contact with nature, however primitive, for nature is by definition the real, and perhaps, in addition, his only real love. It is this deep ambivalence both Frost and Thoreau work out in aspects of their writing at an almost visceral level and with a degree of concreteness that one simply does not find in Emerson. Both are impelled toward experience and yet are intensely aware of its implicit destructiveness to this very self which desires and seeks; they are aware, in other words, that what one will encounter will be a profound alterity to oneself. Yet they feel that this violence is indispensable, a disguised gift-bringer that in the form of opposition and perhaps of suffering, and always in the form of surprise and the unforeseen, brings one the world.

The Abundance of Being and Non-being

I would like to turn to the well-known "After Apple Picking." It too is a poem of enthusiastic transport and *ekstasis,* but as we shall see it manages this with a greater gentleness than we have seen till now and in fact with as astonishing ease.

> My long two-pointed ladder's sticking through a tree
> Toward heaven still,

And there's a barrel that I didn't fill
Beside it, and there may be two or three
Apples I didn't pick upon some bough.
But I am done with apple-picking now.
Essence of winter sleep is on the night,
The scent of apples: I am drowsing off.
I cannot rub the strangeness from my sight
I got from looking through a pane of glass
I skimmed this morning from the drinking trough
And held against the world of hoary grass.
It melted, and I let if fall and break.
But I was well
Upon my way to sleep before it fell,
And I could tell
What form my dreaming was about to take.
Magnified apples appear and disappear,
Stem end and blossom end,
And every fleck of russet showing clear.
My instep arch not only keeps the ache,
It keeps the pressure of a ladder-round.
I feel the ladder sway as the boughs bend.
And I keep hearing from the cellar bin
The rumbling sound
Of load on load of apples coming in.
For I have had too much
Of apple-picking: I am overtired
Of the great harvest I myself desired.
There were ten thousand thousand fruit to touch,
Cherish in hand, lift down, and not let fall.
For all
That struck the earth,
No matter if not bruised or spiked with stubble,
Went surely to the cider-apple heap
As of no worth.
One can see what will trouble
This sleep of mine, whatever sleep it is.
Were he not gone,
The woodchuck could say whether it's like his
Long sleep, as I describe its coming on,
Or just some human sleep.

The opening six lines create a deft metaphor, yet it is designed to convey not only the experience of effort and the joy one might have in it, but also a sense of its limits: there is a barrel still unfilled, apples still left on the bough, and the passage's final line brings the reader up against the idea of termination. Yet the entire section has such ease and grace that it forestalls any sense of failure or insufficiency, and it is clear from the tone and relaxed movement of the verse that the speaker's emotion is one of fulfillment and pleasant fatigue. The underlying idea is of a natural process that has reached its completion and which is simply rounded out with the last line: "But I am done with apple-picking now." The gradual arc of this opening movement is punctuated with the two lines which follow it: "Essence of winter sleep is on the night, / The scent of apples: I am drowsing off." Here the rhythm is more terse, yet still graceful and, if anything, even more like a kind of incantation. In addition, the lines have the effect of shifting the perspective. We suddenly realize that the opening was not a description of an actual activity in the present, but a memory occurring in the speaker's mind, a remembered present which now, in his drowsiness, he relives with uncanny vividness. We will see that this remembering is in effect a repossessing of the initial experience at a deeper level: in such a way that the surfaces of experience are one with its depths.The stem end and blossom end of apples, the sway of the ladder and the pressure of its rungs, and all the various details of picking apples convey an entire sense of human life — a multi-dimensional sensorium — and create a kind of compressed myth in which the nature of physical experience is distilled in its essential form.

The main portion of the dream occurs in lines 9 through 26. The speaker's first memory is one of "strangeness" cast over his sight by looking through a sheet of ice skimmed from a drinking trough. Of course, in reality such "strangeness" would be merely blurriness, yet in the realm of the dream such a blur is necessary and has an important function: that of creating an effect of the uncanny, which is the specific property of the visionary. It is necessary that one's waking mind and its rational ordering be surpassed by the experience of the dream, whose total import necessarily exceeds the demarcations of ordinary reason. Sight is the sense which more than any other orders and demarcates our world for us and allows us to negotiate it, just as it was the one loss Emerson could not imagine any possible compensation for. It is appropriate, therefore, that this sense should be the first to be transformed in order that its rage for order not impede the more significant development of visionary experience. Yet sight is not banished from the poem; rather its capacity for detail is absorbed into the body of the dream through evocative images: "stem end and blossom end, / And every fleck of russet showing clear." This occurs after the "pane of glass" has fallen away, like a partition, and we are admitted into the heart of the poem itself. The following lines, 19 thru 26, are the core of the vision, a re-creation of sensuous experience in which all senses take part. Thus, not only do we see apples, which now are not disposed in the orderly space of normal sight, but rather float and fade before us in a fluid continuum, but we also feel the sway of the ladder, the pressure on the foot of the ladder-round and finally hear the sound of apples tumbling into the bin. All senses have been combined in a complete and non-reductive experience of reality.

Moreover, it is an experience which is full of paradoxes, just as waking experience itself might be seen to be. It is, for instance, a passive experience, and yet at the same time active, for the speaker seems to go through the entire exertion of work all over again. It is a dream, and thus insubstantial and fleeting, yet also marvelously concrete, and in it the *qualia* of experience are brought forward for the dreamer, pressed upon him as it were, and he finds himself possessed by and subjected to them, to their manifold burgeoning even as their simultaneous evanescence is also made palpable. Experience presses upon and dominates the subject, making it feel and perceive (it is not at all a matter of choice) and then disperses, fading as though it were something entirely insubstantial. There is also a sense, curiously, of both objective order and subjective randomness: one image follows another in a fluid montage that is governed by a general narrative but in which time is compressed and in which space is completely grouped around the speaker. At one point — when he hears the rumbling sound of loads of apples coming in — it is as if he has one foot on the ladder and one ear in the cellar simultaneously. Yet there is a sense in which this too mirrors our actual experience in the world, in which we negotiate two spaces and two times at once — the gridded map of the city and the internalized sense of its spatial layout, clock time and internal experiential time. Finally, the passage's emotional tone is not entirely unmixed, since in the suggestion of wear and tear (the instep arch aching) and in the very image of harvest in the concluding lines we find a slight foreshadowing of mortality.

These are picked up and amplified in the poem's next section. By this point the vision is already beginning to fade, so that we no longer have the illusion of immediate experience quite as strongly. The poem changes mode slightly to become a meditation on the nature of that experience. Perhaps it is inevitable that melancholy increases with meditation, and we see that there is a pronounced tone of reconsideration, a kind of sobering up:

For I have had too much
Of apple-picking: I am overtired
Of the great harvest I myself desired.

Certainly there is a sense of joy now mellowed by a feeling of gratitude, of having been blessed: "There were ten thousand thousand fruit to touch / Cherish in hand, lift down, and not let fall." The feelings of completion and fatigue seem to steady the poem as though it might have been in danger of becoming too lyrical. Yet there is a still more significant development: the implicit recognition that the abundance of nature is qualified by loss. Nature is wasteful. It discards apples, plants and animals, whole species, and human beings. This wastefulness, moreover, seems part of its essential character. Frost speaks elsewhere of the "good of waste" and of its being part of "the essence of the scheme" ("The Pod of Milkweed"). Here, in what is certainly one of his most beautiful poems, a poem wonderfully evocative of the joy of earthly existence and of the life of the senses, he yet is inevitably drawn to an awareness of the fragility and precariousness of existence and to the immersion of any one creature — whether human or natural — in a context that vastly exceeds it and that reduces it to insignificance amid a boundless surplus. There is a further paradox to add to those already mentioned, therefore: though the poem seems to present experience as a fullness and to give to it some of the wholeness of an organic process or form, there is yet beneath this or perhaps hidden within it the sense of a formless and ongoing profusion which brings forward existents only to immediately re-submerge them in nothingness.

Thus the poem is built around a curious awareness of limit and boundlessness simultaneously; the limit is of any individual life; the boundlessness the continual profusion of nature that it rests upon and which encompasses it completely. The dream must be resolved, and yet not by awakening from it (for their can be no awakening from existence) but by lapsing into a still deeper sleep where dreams will no longer have any relevance. This deeper sleep is, from one perspective, merely part of the natural process and in fact is the normal state of nature as such, mere insentience. Yet from the sleeper's standpoint it is, of course, death; and not merely death as a natural fact, but as a human fact, the most significant of human existence. The word, tellingly, is not used; yet its substitute "sleep" tolls like a bell three times in the last five lines and is given the last word.

The remarkable thing, however, is the tone: there is no sense of the ominous or the frightening. Quite the opposite in fact, for the poet speaks with a gentleness that suggests a calm and almost casual acquiescence. The very last line is perhaps the most brilliant from this standpoint; it might be seen as an evasion, but it is really an acceptance of mortality so profound that it need not be directly stated. The poet knows quite well what this "human sleep" is, and knows that it is not like the woodchuck's temporary hibernation, for though any given animal must die, it yet does not have to give up a powerfully individualized existence, as a human being must do, and indeed not merely a life but an entire project imbued with self-awareness, and a sense of valuation, and in fact of responsiveness — to others and to the world itself. Woodchucks come and woodchucks go, and if one dies, its replacement is never far away. Every human, though, is unique and somehow exceeds the order of nature through its very awareness of that order, and through its self-awareness. The peculiar pathos of human existence lies in the necessity of giving up precisely this complex fate. Why then is the poet's tone so casual? In a way, it is not. There is an understated sobriety in the conclusion and particularly in the last line, with its calculated tone of certitude masquerading as surmise. Yet the poem's whole emotional ambience forbids an overt gravity. More importantly, an essential part of its meaning is that human death, though of unique importance, is yet also a natural phenomenon as well, and so should proceed as effortlessly as any other. One's life might be seen as having its own organic rhythm of growth, with death simply its ultimate issue: death is not catastrophe but fruition.

This point is best illustrated by a parallel between Frost's poem and two poems by Keats that I have always felt to be present in it as informing spirits, the "Ode to a Nightingale" and "To Autumn." In fact, it is interesting to see the way these two contrary influences play against each other, the one a poem of agony, ecstatic trance and death, the other a descriptive piece, calm and slow with the organic roundedness of natural fulfillment. Ultimately, it is the Nightingale Ode that is the more crucial influence; like it, "After Apple-Picking" deals with the death of the poet. Both are a kind of soliloquy undertaken as the speaking subject enters a retrospective twilight prior to passing out of existence completely. Yet Frost's poem is utterly free of the romantic agony that is so overwhelming in Keats. Though the subject is his own death, he writes about it with great ease. It is as though he rewrites the Nightingale ode in the mood of "To Autumn." Of course, a comparison with this latter piece might not be surprising, since both poems deal with harvest and have obvious similarities on the level of imagery: they are both celebrations of natural plenitude and both move slowly through a process of graduated transitions toward a resolving quiet. The parallel with the Nightingale Ode is perhaps less obvious. Yet both it and "After Apple-Picking" begin with a sense of satiation. The speaker in both cases confesses having had enough: in Frost's case of picking apples; in Keats's, of the nightingale's song. There is then a movement of withdrawal away from that external realm and toward a visionary state characterized by a generally heightened perception. In Keats, this begins with stanza four and continues through stanza six:

> Away! away! For I will fly to thee,
> Not charioted by Bacchus and his pards,
> But on the viewless wings of Poesy,
> Though the dull brain perplexes and retards:
> Already with thee! tender is the night,
> And haply the Queen-Moon is on her throne,
> Cluster'd around by all her starry Fays;
> But here there is no light,
> Save what from heaven is with the breezes blown
> Through verdurous glooms and winding mossy ways.
>
> I cannot see what flower are at my feet,
> Nor what soft incense hangs upon the boughs,
> But, in embalmed darkness, guess each sweet
> Wherewith the seasonable month endows
> The grass, the thicket, and the fruit-tree wild;
> White hawthorn, and pastoral eglantine;
> Fast fading violets cover'd up in leaves;
> And mid-May's eldest child,
> The coming musk-rose, full of dewy wine,
> The murmurous haunts of flies on summer eves.

As in Frost, this middle section is the core of the poem, when the poet enters the heightened realm of essences in which nature is perceived more fully and massively than usual. Here Keats's language becomes incredibly lush with a full and resonant diction and a profusion of synesthesia. Again, as in Frost, the intent is to convey an intuitive sense of the total sensuous experience of nature, of the essence of what it is like to be physically alive, by creating a kind of total and virtual sense experience combining, in particular, touch, scent, and hearing. Both pieces, significantly, have an ambivalence with respect to sight; it is partially darkened or veiled in both cases in order to give priority to these other senses.

There are certain other unexpected similarities with Frost. We might point out a remarkable verbal echo, for example: "I cannot see what flowers are at my feet"; and "I cannot rub this strangeness from my sight . . . " These two lines occur at analogous points in their respective poems, when the poet is somewhat far gone in his ecstasy, and the ordinary mode of perception has been left behind in favor of the more inclusive and imaginary one we have noted, based upon a reordering of sense perception, with sight itself either muted (as in Frost) or eclipsed entirely (as in Keats) in order to allow the other senses to function more completely in this complex harmony. This fluid reordering of sensation is itself a paradoxical experience, since it both confirms the self by surfeiting the senses' desire to perceive and yet de-centers it through the very intensity of its reordering. In addition, this muting or loss of sight might be seen as a metaphor for a partial loss of self: an eclipse of the eye, standing for a partial loss of "I." Indeed, in contrast with Frost, Keats experiences a complete suppression of sight, his eye is totally quenched in "embalmed darkness," and it is he who also seems to undergo the most complete disordering of self. There is even a certain quality of swooning in his poem that is quite the opposite of Frost's balance and control. There are then clear structural similarities between the two poems — despite differences in tone — and both treat similar themes: the poet's imagination of his own death.

Moreover, they both turn upon an essential problem inherent in this theme, that of the need to submit to a loss of self, or of how such a loss can be imagined: in Keats this is attended by a profound agony; in Frost it is handled with grace and aplomb with only the slightest trace of pathos. Frost's remarkable achievement is to have handled the theme of the extinction of selfhood with a calculated ease and to have included in this some of the same sense of natural fulfillment which we find in a poem like "To Autumn." "After Apple-Picking" has always struck me as one of the greatest short poems in the language, and we can get some sense of its almost miraculous brilliance by considering that what it took Keats two different poems to express Frost seems able to accomplish in one.[4]

Of course, to view death as a natural fruition is hardly natural, however much such a view might employ organic metaphors. Everyone is aware that death does not generally proceed that way. Yet we must recognize that the poet seeks to create a myth and that its purpose is to suggest a certain type of insight, a certain disposition toward the world and toward one's own experience. We recall the lines which announced the beginning of the dream proper: "Essence of winter sleep is on the night, / The scent of apples: I am drowsing off." In a way these are the most remarkable lines of the poem and give a kind of synopsis of the whole. The first line, at any rate, is certainly the most striking, and the only obviously "poetic" one. What is "Essence of winter sleep" and how is it "on the night?" And what does the scent of apples have to do with it, or for that matter with drowsing off? The lines are almost free association, yet one instinctively accepts them. The reason, aside from their intrinsic beauty, lies in the imagination's willingness to accept the idea of a "something" involving cold and darkness and associated with the dormancy of winter. At this point in the poem, the speaker intuits this aspect in nature and represents it as an essence, a knowable "something" perhaps akin to the "something" that did not love walls in "Mending Wall." Now it is vaguely associated with the fecundity of nature, as opposed to its disruptive power. Deleuze, for instance, calls attention to the early natural philosophy developed in Stoic thought, in which, in a kind of anticipation of process philosophy and Merleau-Ponty's phenomenology, positive being was attributed to qualities as well as to substance itself.

> In Aristotle . . . all categories are said of Being; and difference is present in Being, between substance as the primary sense and the other categories which are related to it as accidents. For the Stoics, on the other hand, states of affairs, quantities, and qualities are no less beings (or bodies) than substance is; they are a part of substance, and in this sense they are contrasted with an *extra-Being* which constitutes the incorporeal as a nonexisting entity. The highest term therefore is not Being, but *Something (aliquid)*, insofar as it subsumes being and non-being, existence and inherence.
>
> (*The Logic of Sense*, 6-7)

The something, the *aliquid*, an idea we encountered before in looking at "Mending Wall," is beyond both being and non-being. As such it is a kind of basis or support for both. We might see a similar intuition in Frost's lines — there is an ultimate yet enigmatic substratum to natural life which yet cannot be named and which is not capturable through specific images. Moreover, it includes both presence and absence, both Being and Nothingness, and hence can be (slightly) imagined in terms of sense impressions — particularly of a vague and non-visual kind ("the scent of apples") or of an abstract kind ("essence of winter sleep") — and absence as such (the overall darkness the lines imply and then name as "the night"). We see again, therefore, just as we saw before in "Mending Wall," the poet's imagination attempting to grasp the essential nature of existence and intuitively proposing a "something" lying beyond or behind natural phenomena, a something which yet defeats representation (and still more anthropocentric or anthropomorphic patterns of thought).

And yet in the very next lines we are returned to the realm of sense impressions and concrete experience. It is as if we were not prepared to face this essence of winter sleep just yet. In order to do so, we will have to go through the total experience of life all over again, dream through it in detail before we can finally encounter "winter sleep" in a definitive way at the end. When we do, and when we have uncovered the underlying character of experience, then we will be able to face the human sleep which awaits us. The character of experience is, as we have seen, something paradoxical, and now we can recognize its essential features more clearly. It is an experience of plenitude and yet of insubstantiality, of organic form and of temporal process, of individuating limit and yet of boundlessness, of endless surfaces (images) welling up out of bottomless depths which we suspect to be yet more surfaces. It partially creates the self, forming it out of these images, yet it draws it out of itself as well, drawing it outward eventually into a nocturnal space of dream and ultimate extinction. Emerson speaks of human power being "not in longevity but in removal." In this poem we glimpse the possibility of an experience in which one might feel that one was undergoing the final uncovering of the nature of experience as such which one had been progressively working toward all one's life. It is as if we are peeling away the layers of our experience in the world, layer by layer, working toward a more naked encounter with the essence of human existence. The poem is finally concerned to give us our own experience in the world in a heightened and clarified form and does this by placing us imaginatively at just that point when we are leaving the world.

Conclusion

"To Earthward" and "After Apple-Picking" are poems that deal with the nature of selfhood and experience and with ways the self can actively possess its own experience and discover its own nature. Yet in the attempt to break through to the actual character of experience, these poems uncover the fact of mortality as well. Our effort to know some reality outside of ourselves, to genuinely experience the world and to feel possessed of such a capacity even as we exercise it, forces us to recognize the necessity of relinquishing the self that we already are. We come to realize that death is not wholly "other"; it cannot be seen as something entirely foreign which breaks in upon us. Rather, it is implied in all our experience and gives it significance.

The poems work out these concerns by means of a paradoxical dynamic. Both, as they unfold, describe a loss of self, a transport or ecstatic state. In "To Earthward" this is manifest as a sudden eruption of evocative imagery. In "After Apple-Picking" this loss of self is announced with the onset of the dream state. Yet both poems temper this ecstasy through a controlling impulse which preserves or confirms selfhood. In "To Earthward" this can be seen as the element of will or ferocity that we spoke of. Likewise, "After Apple-Picking" exhibits a deftness and poise which bespeaks a balanced though precarious control that tempers the poem's power of reverie, directing it in part to the reconstitution of sense experience and its deeper and fuller enjoyment by the dreaming subject and hence toward a confirmation of that subject, even as it prepares this subject for its final removal, its human sleep. Both poems embody paradoxes, though they ultimately are concerned to move beyond the self and realize that selfhood as such must be superceded. They also recognize that it must not be *violated.* One must move beyond it through a complex strategy of simultaneous accomplishment and renunciation. Neither piece is one of Dionysian excess. The final realization toward which both poems move involves not merely the loss of self, but its simultaneous loss and confirmation. Death annihilates me; yet it also confirms my selfhood even as it does so, for, as Heidegger insists, it is always mine and can in no way be delegated. It is in this peculiar sense the deepest confirmation of my separate existence as a distinct individual. Yet the same might be said of all concrete experience. Death only exhibits this fact in its most extreme form. All the rest of our concrete life is continually telling us the same thing, though in ways so ordinary that we overlook them — we gain our life by giving it up . This is why a poem like "After Apple-Picking" is so subtly luminous. We need not live continually estranged from our most concrete experience, from our life itself. Even the most common act can be relived and more deeply experienced through the imagination. By this means we penetrate its true significance and discover the roots of our experience. They lie in our cherishing of the world and working in it, even as it slips by on its temporal passage, and they lie also in the process of our living acts by which we bring ourselves and the world into being, yet on the crest of whose wave we are moved along toward death. Both "To Earthward" and "After Apple-Picking" show us that it is the ardent and poised riding of a wave that our life must be seen to be.

CHAPTER FOUR

Place

Is the world a place of light or is it one of darkness? Is it a world of color or one of gray on gray? Are humans capable of knowing it truthfully, whether in its detail or in its totality? The exquisite complexity of style which balances a desire for beauty and a need to insure the accuracy of a tactful contact with the world reveals also the way the world exceeds any description of it, and reveals as well the inherent delicacy of its balances and orders. In the world of work, a world which humans must construct in order to survive, the fragility and dependencies their material condition forces upon them are seen to coexist with a potential for violence; at the same time, the constructions they create are also threatened by the forces of nature itself, which disrupt and disperse them. And yet humans themselves, for better or for worse, are always at the center of their own world. Accordingly, we looked carefully at two poems that dramatize in particularly distilled form the nature of their powerful inner life. Yet they showed the self in its very self-exceeding, in its eroticism and its mortality, and thus created a picture of a radically unstable entity whose existence is a continual exposure and lability.

There is, however, a further dependency and this is the fragility of the understanding itself and of the shifting borders where it meets the actual, and thus the uncertainty by which it remains in contact with it. Though there is a progressively deepening encounter with otherness, there is also a questioning of knowledge, of its nature and its conditions. In addition, social relations which we saw to be fragile in the sense of being always subject to the disruptions and irruptions of passions and violence are endangered too by another factor operating from within, this tendency of the mind — perhaps especially marked during times of stress or in periods of prolonged and profound isolation — to disintegrate into wandering and disconnected thoughts, into mere fantasies, and aimless waiting. Our purpose in this chapter is to examine some of the ways the human person dramatically enacts its connection to the external world and to assess some of the most prominent factors that endanger or impair that connection, whether internal or external.

Finally, we must ask what is the picture of the world these encounters create in their sum?

We might begin with a topic that seems especially indicative of the human relationship with the external world. This is the relation to and depiction of landscape, for this seems to focus, as though in exemplary instances, many of the issues I want especially to examine. Before proceeding to Frost's interesting treatment of this subject, however, I would like to consider some remarks on Thoreau that can serve to illustrate a number of important contrasts between Frost and much of the rest of the American tradition that precedes him. This will help to focus some of the particular characteristics of Frost's vision. Consider, for example, Frederick Garber's comments on Thoreau:

> all the lines that bisect experience shoot out from the site he [Thoreau] occupies, which means that the position of the observer is the central point from which all directions flow. Genius, the element of pure Being, sits immovably at that still point, while talent moves out along the radii into the world of experience. Thoreau's conception of centrality is deeper than all the moral implications which a Transcendentalist would draw from it concerning man's key position in the universe. Indeed, the relation of centrality to some accepted Transcendental doctrines is only one factor in explaining its importance to him, and it is not the most important one. Thoreau's perception of the centrality of the self, or of an aspect of the self, was one of the major determining principles in the way his consciousness perceived and ordered experience, and it was so in a way that transcended local influences. All Thoreauvian perception begins from his awareness of the point of self shooting out radii, or from its alternate in which the point where consciousness begins is at the exact center of some enclosure, often but not exclusively a sphere. (*Thoreau's Redemptive Imagination*, 4)

And further:

> the point of centrality is locative; when I know where it is I can say that here is my pure center, this is where I am. . . . The move to Walden Pond, the clearing of the land and the building of the house, was in great part an effort by Thoreau to find out where he was, — "where I lived." His imagination was extraordinarily visual and kinesthetic, which meant that when he wanted to locate his own place, or set up the process by which he could search for it, the activity of locating had to be put into graphic, physical terms. He had to build something and clear something else, to work hard on an object or place that could be seen by himself and others. (5-6)

Yet these remarks point out a fundamental impulse not only in Thoreau but also in an array of American writers. One thinks perhaps especially of Whitman who, in "Crossing Brooklyn Ferry," sees spokes of light raying outward from his own head reflected in the water. Perhaps we can locate the impulse in painting too, in the classic American depictions of landscape of the Hudson River School which place the viewer at the focal point of sight lines reaching out into an enormously deep horizon joined to a seeming infinity of sky, with yet no loss of clarity and with an almost Pre-Raphaelite feeling for detail. The American gaze wants indeed to own the landscape, to move out into it and to take possession of it in all its physical reality; and the American act which follows that gaze is a physical taking possession. It is strange, in fact, the degree to which Frost actually avoids participating in this tradition, though it must be said that *ownership* seems everywhere present in the universe he creates, seems to be one of its inescapable givens. Yet Frost, in my view, crucially does not see humans as occupying a central place in the world. Perhaps for this reason there is a hesitancy and a tentativeness about his representations of landscape. Though he could in fact write poems celebrating the American appropriation of an entire continent, "The Gift Outright," for example, there is another sense in which his imagination shrank from such expansions (and expansionism). Though his overtly expressed politics are at times reactionary, perhaps a truer sense of the political implications of his work is to be found in this impulse of tentativeness, uncertainty, and awareness of limits and of the perils of overreaching.

Yet to begin with we might start with a piece that foregrounds, as though in a pure and rather abstract form, the basic issues of how the self relates to its environment, attempting to know it and to shape it.

Center, Circumference, and Ray of Relation

In "Beech," a late poem, he exhibits about as much certainty and confidence as his inherent skepticism and caution would allow.

BEECH

Where my imaginary line
Bends square in woods, an iron spine
And pile of real rocks have been founded.
And off this corner in the wild,
Where these are driven in and piled,
One tree, by being deeply wounded,
Has been impressed as Witness Tree
And made commit to memory
My proof of being not unbounded.

Thus truth's established and borne out,
Though circumstanced with dark and doubt —
Though by a world of doubt surrounded.

In this poem the mind reaches out into the physical world to see to what extent it can orient itself there and, beyond that, to determine the degree to which it can control and shape that world. The opening lines clearly suggest this. It is as though the poet is reaching out to take control and to manage the environment, albeit in a purely visualized gesture: his imaginary line marks off a certain portion of the surrounding woods, and one can imagine him physically orienting himself according to this mental action and the imaginary demarcation it has made. Yet this act of mind is insufficient in itself; it must be supported by a real act. Where the imaginary line goes, physical labor must follow and build an actual marker to supplement the act of mental definition:

an iron spine
And pile of real rocks have been founded.

The poem thus far concerns the way mentality can impress itself upon the physical world in an effort to make it more manageable and more comprehensible. On one level, the theme is similar to Stevens's "Anecdote of the Jar" which made the slovenly wilderness surround the hill where it was placed and so introduced an element of order and coherence into the landscape. Yet Stevens's poem remains always on the level of thought — parable, meditation, argument. Frost starts with this, but he quickly moves to the realm of action, attempting to indicate an organic relation between the two. In this piece, the testing movement of imagination must be ratified by the physical effort of actually shaping the world. The imagination's constructs can only be valid if they take account of the real, and this they cannot do if confined entirely to the hypothetical. They must rather be tested through a kind of agonistic relation to the world itself. This process is not shown, of course, but its necessity is implied in the writing itself, in both substance and manner. And we may even notice a somewhat resolute tone in the verse with its emphatic syntax and prominent rhymes, as well as its diction suggesting the clash of effort and resistance:

And off this corner in the wild,
Where these are driven in and piled,
One tree, by being deeply wounded,
Has been impressed as Witness Tree
And made commit to memory
My proof of being not unbounded.

Yet having said this, we must also remember that the imaginative act did come first, giving direction and purpose to the real actions that would follow. We touch here upon a motive for physical work well beyond that of physical necessity. There is a human need to create intellectual order and then to physically inscribe it in the world. The poem, therefore, sketches the ideal interaction of person and environment: a visualizing act of mind creates an implicit human project which then moves outward into the real world, intersecting with it and shaping it. Yet there is a strange loneliness in the poem as well, for the only witness to this act is the tree itself.[1] Nature is empty of any spirits, of any gods or God who might witness; and here at least it would likewise seem to be empty of other people. The poem is a parable about the human condition itself in which self and world encounter each other in an essential solitude. Indeed, though the poet wishes to emphasize the capacity of mind and body to comprehend reality and to shape it, he yet is aware of the dark and ambiguous substratum on which the poem's confident affirmation rests, and the essential isolation of its protagonist.

The final lines give expression to this aspect of things: truth, though tested and borne out, is circumstanced with darkness. "Circumstanced" is an apt choice of words, indicating as it does both physical encirclement and a deeper existential situation of ambiguity and latent threat which is always the case whether we are physically encircled or not, and whether we clearly realize it or not. The last line simply repeats this meaning, but with a beautiful and musical redundancy which invests the point with a grave and thoughtful cadence. In a way, then, we might even go so far as to say that the poet's intention is to draw our awareness as much to that circumscribing doubt as to the resistant powers of imagination, will, and effort, for we may be even more inclined to lose sight of it and the dark realities which elicit it. And yet as we step back from the poem for a moment, we can see that the overall import is focused on the effort to hold these two principles in view simultaneously: to make us more fully aware of our ability to know the world and to shape it, yet, beyond that, to make us more alert to the difficulties inherent in this and of the limits within which we must work. These limits comprise human finitude itself, as well as the essential isolation of every individual from every other. Yet here it is this balancing itself, this austere rectitude, as we might think of it, which takes precedence and which rises up austerely in the poem into a pure and empty light.

Scapeland

We must turn to "The Wood Pile" for a fuller treatment of these intertwined themes of the human desire to know and order the world and the attendant sense of human finitude and loneliness. The opening third of the poem presents us with a bleak landscape that the speaker must traverse. Our first impression is one of being brought into the situation *in medias res*; there is no opening gesture or preparatory statement. We are suddenly "there" along with him:

Out walking in the frozen swamp one gray day,
I paused and said, "I will turn back from here.
No, I will go on farther — and we shall see."
The hard snow held me, save where now and then
One foot went through. The view was all in lines
Straight up and down of tall slim trees
Too much alike to mark or name a place by
So as to say for certain I was here
Or somewhere else: I was just far from home.

The question, is where are we? The landscape is devoid of any distinctive feature, or indeed of any interest or attraction. It would appear that the speaker is himself somewhat puzzled. There is a momentary hesitation in the opening line; he pauses to get his bearings, wonders if he should turn around, and then decides to go on. Yet he is not able to get his bearings completely, and does not clearly know where he is. "I paused and said, 'I will turn back from here. / No, I will go on farther — and we shall see.'" We have the impression of a resolute speaker who seems in some way determined to get something out of this perplexing encounter. He therefore pushes ahead despite uncertainties and possible dangers. He does not know what he will find in his errand into this wilderness, whether something great, small, or nothing whatever. Yet he is decisive in wanting to continue. Perhaps there is a primitive desire just to see, to know the world and to know what it is for no other reason than the fact that one is in it. We might think of this as the curiosity that pulls one forward from day to day, though in fact they may be nothing but a succession of "gray days." It is such curiosity, too, that writers of fiction manipulate to capture our interest and make us wonder what will happen next. The word "interest" itself means "to be in the midst of." And if we are in suspense, we are literally hanging, suspended. So far in the poem Frost has skillfully made us experience what it is like to be suspended in such uncertainties and the way in which it makes us cast ahead in an attempt to see what is coming next. And yet, strangely, as soon as our interest *is* caught by the opening, we are led along a path which, far from amplifying or exploiting our suspense, seems to dissipate it in a remarkably uneventful development:

The hard snow held me, save where now and then
One foot went through. The view was all in lines
Straight up and down of tall slim trees
Too much alike to mark or name a place by
So as to say for certain I was here
Or somewhere else: I was just far from home.

This landscape is leveled, both physically and from the standpoint of narrative. It is as if all hierarchies have been omitted or rejected; nothing is more important than anything else, nothing takes logical precedence. The speaker moves over the landscape in a meandering and almost pointless way. Details are brought to our attention not for their narrative potential, but in a purely phenomenological way, for the way they have of filling in the perceptible world immediately before the speaker. As a world, it is fairly monochromatic. If one had to illustrate the poem, one could do so using only varying shades of gray with perhaps a little brown and black here and there. Indeed it is important to recognize this monotony of color, for it has an epistemological significance, besides merely contributing to the atmosphere. In the poem the entire phenomenal world presents itself in terms of vaguely differentiated areas of gray which shade off into each other: the lighter gray of the snow and frozen water becomes a somewhat darker gray of bare trees which in turn are seen against the background of a gray sky. In such a context, demarcation becomes uncertain. Thus through this color scheme alone, subtle elements of description become a means for suggesting problems of knowledge; in this case, that of the difficulty of making clear boundary distinctions in nature and hence of distinguishing any given entity from the surrounding context in which it is seen.

We can find a similar vision in A. R. Ammons's poem, "Corsons Inlet":

manifold events of sand
change the dune's shape that will not be the same shape
tomorrow,

so I am willing to go along, to accept
the becoming
thought, to stake off no beginnings or ends, establish
        no walls:

by transitions the land falls from grassy dune to creek
to undercreek: but there are no lines, though
        change in that transition is clear
        as any sharpness: but "sharpness" spread out,
allowed to occur over a wider range
than mental lines can keep . . .

Here likewise it is impossible to mark out any given thing in a definite way; it can be done only provisionally, and it is the recognition of this provisionality of interpretation which Ammons's poem explicitly urges on the reader at its conclusion:

> I see narrow orders, limited tightness, but will
> not run to that easy victory:
> still around the looser, wider forces work:
> I will try
> to fasten into order enlarging grasps of disorder, widening
> scope, but enjoying the freedom that
> Scope eludes my grasp, that there is no finality of vision,
> that I have perceived nothing completely,
> that tomorrow a new walk is a new walk.

Frost might well agree with this attitude, but in "The Wood-Pile" at least, he is more concerned with assessing its cost than Ammons appears to be. Frost's speaker seems to be aware that it is not a simple matter to let go of all certainties of interpretation; indeed, if one were in the middle of a frozen swamp, it could be a matter of life and death. Frost's inherently dramatic approach makes us aware of the potential difficulties of such negative capability at the most concrete level. Thus, the sense of being lost, of being physically and mentally at risk, is brilliantly conveyed by the passage about the woods themselves:

> The view was all in lines
> Straight up and down of tall slim trees
> Too much alike to mark or name a place by
> So as to say for certain I was here
> Or somewhere else: I was just far from home.

These lines are perhaps the most succinct poetic presentation of that most characteristic of all modern ideas, the idea of relativity, for they describe a condition in which all basis for measurement and orientation has been lost. Direction and distance are uncertain; and the very idea of place is hard to maintain. It is as if the basic terms by which we orient and direct ourselves are no longer valid, as though the glue which holds the phenomenal world together were loosened, and the constituents of nature — place, time, direction — were set adrift: left and right become uncertain, up and down meaningless, sky is hard to distinguish from earth and one place is much the same as any other. Moreover, all drifts by without orienting incident and presents itself as a vaguely differentiated expanse of gray. We progress from the relative uncertainty of the opening lines to the more profound uncertainty in which the speaker now finds himself, that of relativity itself. Yet despite this radical uncertainty, he pushes on, carrying out the intention of the opening.

Surely there is a certain paradox in this combination of resolve and uncertainty. What does it mean to be possessed of a resolute errancy? Is it not, at last, a metaphor for our human condition itself? And yet it seems that it is easy for us to disguise this very situation, hiding it from ourselves. In the speaker's walk through the frozen swamp, at once purposeful yet with no clear purpose beyond the basic ones of curiosity and a kind of primitive self-assertion too bare of any obvious emotion to appear self-dramatizing, we see another instance of Frost's peculiar combination of a concern with action and an awareness of enigma and existential uncertainty. The author makes us aware of the need to tolerate uncertainties of every kind, yet he also makes us aware of the dangers of this very condition, and, in a way, of its extremity. We must tolerate the enigmatic, and yet there can be no doubt that it endangers us.

This tolerance for the enigmatic is seen even more clearly in the poem's next section. Which presents the piece's only clear incident. It is announced by the speaker when he tells us "A small bird flew before me." By this point those readers who have developed any feeling for the way the poem works will be wary of ascribing any particular significance to the bird, especially since birds frequently come with so many symbolic associations attached. Yet in this perplexing realm, it is best to simply take things at their surface appearance. This appearance is somewhat difficult to guess, however, since we are not given much in the way of description other than the observation that the bird has a white feather in its tail. Apparently, it flits about too rapidly and is too concealed by the trees for the speaker to describe it in more detail. Yet, though the bird is elusive, the speaker seems quite attentive to it and in fact provides us with an extended commentary on it:

> A small bird flew before me. He was careful
> To put a tree between us when he lighted,
> And say no word to tell me who he was
> Who was so foolish as to think what *he* thought.
> He thought that I was after him for a feather —
> The white one in his tail; like one who takes
> Everything said as personal to himself.
> One flight out sideways would have undeceived him.

The rather fanciful nature of these characterizations and the speaker's self-conscious awareness of this make the passage almost a sort of anti-description. Instead of attempting to put before us what the bird looks like, Frost gives us a passage so obviously fanciful that it tends to make us aware of the contrived nature of all representation and the uncertain basis of interpretation. The need for persuasive interpretations is a craving that must be tempered, and the poem is devoted in part to stripping away illusions of control. Definite description, we are made to realize, is itself a type of control, a type of fixing, and the desire for it is part of a quest for certainty which the poem seems to be directed against. The self must be divested of these supports and pared down to a circumspect but alert witnessing. At the same time, the bird represents all the puzzling elements in nature which confound our explanations and expectations but which nonetheless lure us on. It is a teasing and elusive presence. Yet even to say this is to say too much, since the creature is one we barely see and learn of almost entirely at second hand, through the interposed veil of commentary which the poet devises and whose arbitrary and anthropomorphizing character he makes us see. Indeed we come to "see" that, more than the bird itself.

There is a parallel with "Mending Wall," since there too the speaker learned of the forces that were disrupting the wall only in a highly mediated fashion and had to fill in the gaps in his direct knowledge with surmise. Yet there, amid a social context, an encompassing community of interpretation mitigated his encounter with the enigmatic "something." This was a mixed blessing, since that interpretive community (the brute neighbor) was itself part of the problem. Yet it did at least make the experience of the world less stark by including others in it, though these others brought with them a potential for violence that gave the whole piece a tense, though repressed, drama. In this poem, by contrast, there is only the speaker's voice inhabiting the enormous and eerie silence of the swamp. The atmosphere is much less tense, but more stark and denuded of affect, of humanity. There is an absolute loneliness and a peculiar silence in it, a silence which so pervades the poem and seems so naturally a part of the world it depicts that only later do we realize that this bird seems not to have any song and seems not to generate any noise as it flits about from branch to branch.

Since we started this chapter with comparisons to Thoreau, we might recall the section in *Walden* where the narrator encounters the loon. There a definite relationship, and a rather comic one, was established between a human being and the representative of an alien realm — the diving, flying, and quite vocal water bird, which in all its antics was no more accessible than Frost's unnamed bird, but which seemed to address itself more directly to the human presence which had invaded its domain, its world. There is a dramatic aspect to the encounter: animal and human seemed ranged across from each other in the context of a landscape correspondingly clear and available to perception even in its mistiness. In Frost's poem, by contrast, the world itself seems to shift with every step, and there is an absence of reciprocity between animal and human, as likewise between the human and the landscape itself, for there would be no possibility of taking up an abode amid this frozen swamp.

The journey which the poem describes is in fact one of divestiture, a stripping away of the conventional responses by which the external world is explored and comprehended. The speaker must give up the desire to control his surroundings or to feel that he has fixed any part of the world in a clear definition or description. Likewise he must give up the idea that the world in any of its aspects or events is in any way addressed to him. Although an exploratory impulse remains, what it turns up reveals how little the lack of epistemological certainty is merely an epistemological problem, and to what extent it undermines all aspects of human experience, by bringing human limitation to the foreground. In doing so it tends to make human effort appear insignificant. Here we see the quiet extremity of the poem: it seems intended to explore the limits of human experience, to force us into the waste places of the human universe. We may ask, then, what is in these waste places? What does this trek through the swamp finally reveal? He finds a rotting pile of wood that someone (no one knows who) had chopped and then simply left (no one knows why.) The lines in which the poet states this are eloquent in their complete refusal to elaborate or provide more information than is immediately before him:

> And then there was a pile of wood for which
> I forgot him and let his little fear
> Carry him off the way I might have gone,
> Without so much as wishing him good-night.
> He went behind it to make his last stand.
> It was a cord of maple, cut and split
> And piled — and measured, four by four by eight.
> And not another like it could I see.
> No runner tracks in this year's snow looped near it.
> And it was older sure than this year's cutting,
> Or even last year's or the year's before.
> The wood was gray and the bark warping off it
> And the pile somewhat sunken. Clematis
> Had wound strings round and round it like a bundle.
> What held it, though, on one side was a tree
> Still growing, and on one a stake and prop,
> These latter about to fall. I thought that only

Someone who lived in turning to fresh tasks
Could so forget his handiwork on which
He spent himself, the labor of his ax,
And leave it there far from a useful fireplace
To warm the frozen swamp as best it could
With the slow smokeless burning of decay.

Here finally the revelation we are given is merely a vision of entropy. Yet far from feeling this to be an absurd anti-climax (as it might be in the hands of a less skillful writer), we are left with a sense of the finality of disintegration, and beyond that of the complete futility of human effort, and of the irrelevance of human beings to the natural world. It is as if all the noise and effort of human life is silenced by this one mute image that the poet allows to remain stark and unadorned, this mere pile of old dead wood.

Remarkably, Frost is perfectly at ease in the face of such a terminal vision, and the tone remains as level as it has been throughout the poem, with the poet offering nothing in the way of compensatory gestures. This complete absence of ceremonial tone contrasts with the usual practice of, for example, graveyard meditations or other meditations on mortality which attempt to memorialize a defunct human presence. Nothing like that is really present here. It is as if the speaker has walked beyond the bounds of conventional sentiment. He has, in fact, walked to the edge of the realm of human concern, into an area where the irrelevance of human beings is everywhere evident, and where elegy is impossible. There are a number of disturbing perceptions in this poem, and of these the vision of entropic disintegration is certainly one; yet the last, and perhaps the most disturbing of all, is of the complete irrelevance of elegy. The final image Frost gives us is more enigmatic and troubling, suggesting the complete superceding of everything we think of as human, and of the irrelevance of human projects to the world as it exists in its complete independence of us.

I, Other, Annihilation: Radical Loneliness

And yet we must still, and once again, attend to ourselves. For we are always the center point of any landscape we inhabit. A certain humanism is likewise always present in Frost's work, even when his writing moves into such excursions as we see in "The Wood-Pile," which give external accounts of the estrangement of humans from the natural world, accounts in which it is described from the outside. But what is happening inside? What is the nature of the particular loneliness that permeates a poem like "The Wood-Pile"?

"Acquainted with the Night" is one of Frost's poems that even those who do not generally admire his work often appreciate. They do so most likely for its terse and forceful style and the rhetorical conciseness with which it expresses feelings of anomie and desperation. Indeed, in its nearly histrionic character, it is unique among Frost's poems and is one of the few poems he wrote which seem conspicuously of their time even in outward form and manner, for it is as much a poem of the Age of Anxiety as anything by Eliot or by Auden himself. Yet here the anxiety has a completely existential source and is not particularly tied to social conditions or factors.

ACQUAINTED WITH THE NIGHT

I have been one acquainted with the night.
I have walked out in rain — and back in rain.
I have outwalked the furthest city light.

I have looked down the saddest city lane.
I have passed by the watchman on his beat
And dropped my eyes, unwilling to explain.

I have stood still and stopped the sound of feet
When far away an interrupted cry
Came over houses from another street,

But not to call me back or say good-by;
And further still at an unearthly height
One luminary clock against the sky

Proclaimed the time was neither wrong nor right.
I have been one acquainted with the night.

Perhaps the poem's finest stanza is its very first: the diction is direct and firm, and the rhythm appropriately terse. The breaking of the second line with a pronounced caesura to reinforce the sense creates a particularly strong effect: back and forth, forth and back, the poet has paced the length and breadth of this emptiness which he merely calls "the night" and which, in a particularly telling understatement, he says he is "acquainted with." The suggestion is one of desperation combined with an almost savage restlessness, as if the speaker were a caged animal of some kind.

Yet what is he caged by? We must read further for the answer, though at first we do not find it. Rather, the poem continues with a sequence of increasingly melodramatic images that heighten the mood of isolation and add to it a sense of grimness and foreboding:

I have passed by the watchman on his beat
And dropped my eyes, unwilling to explain.

I have stood still and stopped the sound of feet
When far away an interrupted cry
Came over houses from another street,

But not to call me back or say good-by . . .

Such lines almost suggest the world of Munch. The "interrupted cry" coming out of nowhere "over houses from another street" and left totally unexplained seems particularly daring and successful. In the poem as a whole the images have a cumulative effect, massing as though in successive waves, stanza by stanza. The climax comes with the final image, that of the "luminary clock against the sky." Here the purpose is no longer to heighten the emotional intensity but to provide clarification, a sense of why the speaker is so anxious, agonized, and restless. Our understanding of the poem depends upon this answer, and so in a sense the poem needs no interpretation, since it gives us the answer as plainly as we could wish. We are told "the time was neither wrong nor right." This is clearly an expression of complete relativism, just as the description of the frozen swamp was in "The Wood-Pile." Yet here the situation is portrayed as much less tolerable, for we realize that it is this which the speaker is caged by, quite simply his own radical freedom, which in his present state he experiences as paralyzing and isolating in a particularly intense way.

Part of the reason for the difference in emotional tone between this poem and "The Wood-Pile" can be seen when we consider that here it is orientation in time which is undermined, rather than orientation in space. That is, we might take the phrase "the time was neither wrong nor right" to be more than a metaphor for a general relativism, but to also indicate something about the concrete experience of the speaker: specifically, that he has lost the inherent sense of continuity which enables us to order our inner life by relating our experiences to each other. We might think of this as a sense of temporal coherence: the periods of our experience, day-to-day and week-to-week, are felt as connected in some way. This sense of time is internal and bears upon our ability to feel experience as a comprehensible process with periods of stress and abatement, tension and resolution. Every musician knows that a disruption of a piece's rhythm is the quickest way of derailing it. We might say then that removing the individual's way of giving temporality meaning is just as disruptive. From this standpoint, therefore, the speaker describes a crisis that bears upon his capacity to relate his experiences to others. This creates an anxiety that is conveyed with a remarkable intensity, though its precise occasion is left unspecified.

Yet we have a few clues on this point. For the poem seems to turn around a partially acknowledged sense of guilt. There is a fairly clear suggestion of this in a line like "And dropped my eyes, unwilling to explain," and more clearly in line ten, which describes the strange cry as being not, at any rate, "to call me back or say good-by." A troubled sense of responsibility seems to be concealed in the poem, though it is impossible to elucidate its cause. The very selfhood which feels itself adrift in time, and as a result begins to sense its own disintegration, can at the same time harbor an acute sense of being at fault. Though the self which is troubled in its conscience may be losing its capacity to feel itself integral and whole, it has not lost its capacity to suffer, albeit in a rather spectral fashion.

We can perhaps clarify this if we recall that Levinas proposes that an individual exists in a mode of continually taking up or taking on existence; this movement is itself palpable and in certain experiences it becomes especially clear to awareness. Thus, indolence is explicated as a kind of disinclination before one's own existence, which is experienced as a burden; and in the experience of insomnia this taking up or taking on assumes the form of a kind of pure endurance amid the endless and formless oncoming of the night itself.[2] In this poem by Frost, consciousness becomes acutely aware of its continued burden of self-positing amid a night which is itself without markers or boundaries — except one, of course, the luminous clock which here, now, cannot be other than some sort of *memento mori*. Yet in Levinas we also find the idea that the experience of temporality always requires and contains an experience of the other, a relation to an alterity that calls the individual forth into temporal existence. Temporal existence is, by definition, a being-toward-the-future, yet Levinas, in *Existence and Existents*, understands the future as the possibility of renewal. It could be that this possibility is in some way closed off in the poem and that this has to do specifically with the relation to otherness, and perhaps even to specific others. The speaker, isolated in himself, moves toward an emptiness of time in which there will be only an enduring of pure succession without renewal. It may also be that by appreciating this aspect of this particular poem, we also become aware of a hidden dimension of "The Wood-Pile." For there, although there was certainly an encounter with alterity — the swamp — there was no human otherness to witness, be witnessed by, or address, merely the relic of a past and anonymous effort of physical labor — the wood itself. In this piece, though it is almost equally devoid of others in any real sense, the setting itself — a rare urban setting rather than a rural or wilderness one — makes us aware of the way others are implied in almost every aspect of our being. The sublime isolation of "Beech" and "The Wood-Pile" was perhaps not the ultimate characterization of human existence we might have thought it was.

In its emphasis on the inner experience of time, "Acquainted with the Night" is a threshold conducting us into a special area of Frost's work, a night-world in which the self borders on breakdown and psychosis. We have seen adumbrations of this already in our brief discussion of "A Servant to Servants." Yet this portion of his work also brings forward an interesting emphasis on human sociality and solidarity. Indeed, in at least some of his poetry, Frost shows a response to the hostility of the external world different from that of many other modernist poets.[3] He emphasizes the need for human relatedness, the self's need for others. Specifically, he sees, in the absence of connection to other individuals, the possibility of a gradual lapse into a schizoid state in which the self relates less and less to others but is entirely absorbed in its own processes. We might call this psychosis or schizophrenia, but it is important to realize that there are many degrees and shadings of this condition and that most "normal" persons are vulnerable to this as well, though perhaps less drastically. One of the suggestions the poems I have in mind make, at least to me, is that it may be the continued capacity to relate to others that keeps many people from slipping into the category of the "disturbed." Both the possibility of this and the great importance of ordinary relationships in preventing it have to be seen as fundamental facts in the psychology of human beings and in their moral nature as well.

In a number of Frost's winter poems, in particular, the winter landscape is used to suggest the hostility and indifference of the external world which then must be countered by some force which will tend to preserve the integrity of the human person or of relationships. Yet often these poems dramatize a temptation on the part of a protagonist to withdraw into the self, and the writing seems designed to draw special attention to this tendency. Though a great deal of attention is given in such work to describing this hostile landscape, it is actually this process of withdrawal which is the true danger, since it involves a loss of relatedness to others, as in "An Old Man's Winter Night," where there is no longer any relationship to others at all. Emerson to the contrary, the situation described in his slogan "I and the abyss" is never really viable for human beings. In these poems by Frost we begin to recognize that the "I" is the abyss. In a sense, we can see this all the more clearly since we are not distracted by the more sensational depictions of complete insanity. We recognize that there must be both "I" and "others" if there is to be anything.

The imagery of dark winter nights, of cold and snow is particularly suited to express the idea of a gradual lapse into withdrawal from the external world. In fact, it suggests metaphors which are remarkably similar to those used by R. D. Laing to characterize the experiential world of certain types of psychotic patients. In *The Divided Self* Laing identifies three types of experience basic to many forms of psychosis: engulfment, implosion, petrification and depersonalization:

> A firm sense of one's own autonomous identity is required in order that one may be related as one human being to another. Otherwise, any and every relationship threatens the individual with loss of identity. One form this takes can be called engulfment. In this the individual dreads relatedness as such, with anyone or anything or, indeed, even with himself, because his uncertainty about the stability of his autonomy lays him open to the dread lest in any relationship he will lose his autonomy and identity. . . .
>
> The main manoeuvre used to preserve identity under pressure from the dread of engulfment is isolation. Thus, instead of the polarities of separateness and relatedness based on individual autonomy, there is the antithesis between complete loss of being by absorption into the other person (engulfment), and complete aloneness (isolation). . . . There are many images used to describe related ways in which identity is threatened, . . . e.g. being buried, being drowned, being caught and dragged down into quicksand. . . .
>
> *Implosion*
>
> This is the strongest word I can find for the extreme form of what Winnicott terms the *impingement* of reality. Impingement does not convey, however, the full terror of the experience of the world as liable at any moment to crash in and obliterate all identity . . . The individual feels that, like the vacuum, he is empty. But this emptiness is him. Although in other ways he longs for the emptiness to be filled, he dreads the possibility of this happening because he has come to feel that all he can be is the awful nothingness of just this very vacuum. Any 'contact' with reality is then in itself experienced as a dreadful threat because reality, as experienced from this position, is necessarily *implosive* and thus . . . *in itself* a threat to what identity the individual is able to suppose himself to have. . . .
>
> *Petrification and depersonalization*
>
> In using the term "petrification," one can exploit a number of the meanings embedded in this word:
>
> 1. A particular form of terror, whereby one is petrified, i.e. turned to stone.
> 2. The dread of this happening: the dread, that is, of the possibility of turning . . . from a live person into a dead thing . . . an *it* without subjectivity. . . . (Laing 45-47)

With these descriptions in mind we might turn to three poems which together mark out a range of possible human response to the foreignness of the world. They move along a continuum from subtle dissociation of self from others to severe withdrawal. It is worth repeating that none of these poems represents what would usually be described as "insanity" and that precisely this is part of their value. By refraining from that they prevent us from demonizing psychosis and other dissociative experience, from placing it in an imaginative space from which we in turn dissociate ourselves. The peculiar human task of staying in meaningful relatedness with others is revealed as being a task, an ongoing project, always endangered by subtle deviations that are internal to it. In the poems that follow, I would like to focus on the subtle suggestiveness by which the author allows us to glimpse the underlying nature of the protagonist's relatedness to others — the degree to which that relatedness is active and productive, versus the degree to which it is becoming hardened or deadened, and the results of this when that does occur.

STORM FEAR

When the wind works against us in the dark,
And pelts with snow
The lower-chamber window on the east,
And whispers with a sort of stifled bark,
The beast,
"Come out! Come out!" —
It costs no inward struggle not to go,
Ah, no!
I count our strength,
Two and a child,
Those of us not asleep subdued to mark
How the cold creeps as the fire dies at length —
How drifts are piled,
Dooryard and road ungraded,
Till even the comforting barn grows far away,
And my heart owns a doubt
Whether 'tis in us to arise with day
And save ourselves unaided.

An "external" reading of "Storm Fear" would see it as expressing a moment of existential panic at nature's hostility and indifference. The panic is there, but it seems to me that it arises more from a sense of isolation inherent in the individual, a tendency toward withdrawal from meaningful relatedness to others. The speaker senses this potential in himself and fears it. Instead of a picture of nature's harshness, the poem presents a good example of Laing's idea of "engulfment," albeit at its beginning stage.

The descriptive surface, with its images of darkness and the steady accumulation of deep snow, and the overall feeling of entrapment the piece conveys, is clearly a good objective correlative for this kind of psychological state. The speaker is not actually alone, of course, but he derives little comfort from the presence of his wife and child. In fact, in the last lines, his anxiety reaches out in imagination past the immediate context to the larger community: "And my heart owns a doubt / Whether 'tis in us to arise with day / And save ourselves unaided." It is in effect a grasping, a need for some wider context of relatedness beyond the immediate one of the isolated family and private farm. Yet nothing is available, and the poem ends on this note of conscious desperation, conscious because the speaker seems fully aware of his situation. The poem presents an early stage in the process of withdrawal, since the speaker is still engaged in his world and is capable of bringing all his intellectual and emotional faculties to bear on it in meaningful activity and thought. (He runs a farm, after all.) The fact that he makes a momentary leap beyond the snowbound farm indicates an imagination that can still transcend its immediate context. In addition, the poem's narrative tone contains an element of irony and grim humor that also indicates that the speaker is not overwhelmed by his situation. The poem does not present the worst, because the speaker has not experienced it. Yet there are suggestions that he has glimpses of it. For example, in the subtlety of the poem's phrasing we see the suggestion of a strange alienation of the speaker from his own wife and child. The phrase "those not asleep" seems odd, given the circumstances; one has the impression that his gaze might be travelling over a crowd of people, strangers to each other and to him, as in a barracks say, or some public conveyance; there is a remoteness in the wording, especially in the use of "those" with its distancing anonymity, so that one is surprised to learn in the next line that he is referring to his own wife and child. In choosing words normally applied to a group of strangers for this intimate context, the poet suggests the isolation of each individual in his or her own separate existence and consciousness; the speaker's own gathering isolation, which seems to steal over him through the course of the description, creates an almost physical distance between him and his family. The brilliant effect of expansion of distance between house and barn in line 15 adds to this impression of island-like isolation.

The positive and negative aspects of the speaker's condition — both the sense that he is still engaged in his world and yet the feeling that the drift toward withdrawal is real and powerful — are delicately balanced in the conclusion. On the positive side is the element of humor, of conscious exaggeration; on the negative side is the real fear of a kind of paralysis described by Laing as "petrification," an inner deadness characteristic of certain forms of psychotic withdrawal. The last lines leave the impression of a speaker poised on a narrow edge with conflicting impulses tending in two different directions.

In "Desert Places" the speaker's potential isolation comes one step closer to being fully realized. The sense of speed conveyed in the opening lines, combined with the repetition and emphatic quality of the first line, creates a feeling of vertigo at the outset which can be seen as an example of Laing's experience of "implosion." This somewhat agitated opening settles down a bit as the speaker takes account of his surroundings. It does not settle to a calm, however, but to a mood of desperation and foreboding. We have to ask what the speaker is anticipating with dread in lines like the following:

> And lonely as it is, that loneliness
> Will be more lonely ere it will be less —
> A blanker whiteness of benighted snow
> With no expression, nothing to express.

Again, an answer is suggested by Laing's account, in the last of his descriptive categories, what he calls "petrification." In this state the patient experiences a loss of emotion, an inner deadness and blankness. It is easy to see the blank landscape of the third stanza, and then the completely dead "empty space" of the last, as objectifications and perhaps premonitions of such a state. Significantly, other people have dropped out of the picture completely, except for the fact that the speaker, speaking in the first person, addresses himself directly to us, so that a certain relatedness to others, if only the others as readers, is implied; yet none are represented in the poem which, empty of human beings, does not provide even the possibility of human relatedness.

In this it contrasts with "Stopping by Woods" in which, though the speaker is alone (except for his horse), he is still part of a social matrix and recognizes this: he knows that someone owns the woods, though he is not certain who. The fact that there's no farmhouse near implies that there could be; it normally would be the occasion for such a stop. (That is what the horse is used to.) And finally he has promises to keep. Actually, the implied relationships form a set which moves from the relatively remote to a mid-range of interactive neighborliness (the farmhouses to which he perhaps delivers groceries and the like), to the intimate — those to whom one makes promises important enough to mention in the meditative mood of the final stanza. Though he is alone at the moment, an entire community is implied in his meditations. In "Desert

Places," however, the speaker seems to be moving away from any relatedness with others. This is the case despite the fact that he is clearly on his way somewhere ("a field I looked into going past . . .). The situation outwardly seems much the same as in "Stopping by Woods," yet the inner experience is the opposite: he dreads an increasing isolation and the inner death (really not too strong a term, considering the poem's images) that goes with that. The poem implies an actual destination for the traveler yet closes off the possibility of meaningful human relationship. Isolation seems to hunt him down and corner him, trapping him in his individuality, an isolation made clearer by the images with which he expresses himself, images which become increasingly empty and vast.

The power of increasing withdrawal comes to an end point in "An Old Man's Winter Night." Certainly this is one of Frost's most beautifully realized poems. Its use of aural as well as visual details makes it extremely atmospheric and gives it a remarkably three-dimensional effect. It seems to be not so much a written text as a virtual world in which a particular form of life is recreated and preserved. The account it gives us is developed with great care. The slow patient description, the scrupulous observation detail by detail, results in a picture that is as powerful as it is quiet and understated. Though it is perfectly natural in its phrasing and movement, it is remarkably intense; there is no wasted space at all, but every moment of the poem is filled with some striking image or metaphor. The result is a work that is seamless and smooth, and yet of great cumulative force.

AN OLD MAN'S WINTER NIGHT

All out-of-doors looked darkly in at him
Through the thin frost, almost in separate stars,
That gathers on the pane in empty rooms.
What kept his eyes from giving back the gaze
Was the lamp tilted near them in his hand.
What kept him from remembering what it was
That brought him to that creaking room was age.
He stood with barrels round him — at a loss.
And having scared the cellar under him
In clomping here, he scared it once again
In clomping off — and scared the outer night,
Which has its sounds, familiar, like the roar
Of trees and crack of branches, common things,
But nothing so like beating on a box.
A light he was to no one but himself
Where now he sat, concerned with he knew what,
A quiet light, and then not even that.

He consigned to the moon — such as she was,
So late-arising — to the broken moon,
As better than the sun in any case
For such a charge, his snow upon the roof,
His icicles along the wall to keep;
And slept. The log that shifted with a jolt
Once in the stove, disturbed him and he shifted,
And eased his heavy breathing, but still slept.
One aged man — one man — can't keep a house,
A farm, a countryside, or if he can,
It's thus he does it of a winter night.

The scene opens with a telling reversal of logic: the out of doors looks in at the old man, rather than he looking out at it. This is reinforced by the fine image of the tilted lamp that ironically prevents him from seeing anything except his own reflection. The next two lines echo the immediately preceding in syntax and rhythm, and make it clear that there is a deeper problem: the sense of bafflement and frustration is more than the result of mere absent-mindedness. The real cause is age, as line seven points out; and by doing so it invests the sense of frustration with an existential significance: the isolation, the awkward hopeless attempt at seeing outside (as though expecting someone) are not accidental but part of the essential character of his life. He is not alone by chance; it has become his entire way of being. The first seven lines, therefore, establish an atmosphere of isolation as well as a subdued tone something like the inner voice of solitary thought. These are then augmented, first by the almost humorous image of searching a blank window, then by the idea of time, and finally by that of mortality. In this way, the poem adds a new dimension of meaning at every line, so that what starts out as a visual image ("All out-of-doors looked darkly in . . . ") becomes a more specific situation (a man trying to see outside) which in turn becomes an illumination of an individual's life and its temporal passage. The opening moves from scene to situation to life in a quiet yet sure way, increasing the emotional resonance step by step, until the muted chiming of "gaze" and "age" quietly locks the process shut with its distant off-rhyme.

The next section begins by confirming the impression of absent-mindedness which had been hinted at in line five. We see it now as a loss of memory. Although it is not something to make too much of, it does suggest a certain disorientation. And if we consider memory one of the ways in which selfhood is integrated, we can then infer a certain weakening or faltering: there is a suggestion that the old man is not in complete possession of his faculties and, by extension, of the surroundings which, as the conclusion states, he does not "keep" but merely occupies. The remarkable choice of "clomping" for a verb in two lines clearly suggests an aimless lurching through rooms which are empty not only because no one else is there, but also because he himself is not completely there. He cannot really be said to dwell in them, for he does not fill them with his presence and make them extensions of himself and of his life. He merely occupies them, and they in turn merely house him like a container. In this way, isolation and disorientation indicate an erosion of will and identity. By contrast, we might consider once again the speaker of "The Wood-Pile" who undergoes a potentially disorienting experience, yet retains his capacity to function through a circumspect yet intense resolve. We saw this as a paradoxical phenomenon, to be sure — a resolute errancy which discovered nothing; yet it did allow the speaker to retain a sense of identity. The very tones of voice communicated through the inflections of the verse seemed to assure us of a human presence. Yet here we do not hear the old man; he is silent, and the only voice in the poem is the subdued voice of the poet who refers to his subject only in the third person. Thus, voiceless and nameless, the old man seems an ever more tenuous presence, and the poem's style and manner of presentation bespeak the emptying out of selfhood which is no longer a presence imbued with dramatic immediacy but a vague and tenuous ghost.

This dissolution can also be felt in the strange sense of time the work exhibits. There is a compression, particularly between lines 14 and 15 where something seems to have been left out; and then again between lines 17 and 18, a juncture which also has the character of an elision. Yet it is clear that this temporal foreshortening is not due to a fullness or activity, but to their opposites. We might say that the poem is in part about the experience of boredom. Time is experienced as an emptiness: any moment is as good as any other; and thus the poem skips ahead at various points, or is vague about the duration of certain episodes. In this limbo all moments have been leveled and so are equally meaningless, interchangeable in the overall temporal blank. Ultimately we realize that we are witnessing the process by which individuality is effaced gradually, just as snow quietly effaces the landscape. By some indeterminate point in this process the old man is reduced to simply making idle noises:

> He stood with barrels round him — at a loss.
> And having scared the cellar under him
> In clomping here, he scared it once again
> In clomping off — and scared the outer night,

> Which has its sounds, familiar, like the roar
> Of trees and crack of branches, common things,
> But nothing so like beating on a box.

Beating on a box is about the only thing one could do in such a circumstance. The image recalls Beckett and is remarkable for the way it expresses the completely accidental character of human consciousness, and the smallness and insignificance of the human presence. Nothing depends on this act; it is entirely gratuitous and is merely an instance of his attempt to retain some sense of coherence — in this case by marking time. It is pointless, of course, since he has lost the capacity to actually make use of the time meted out. In this sense, the gesture remains nothing more than that, though it does furnish the poem with one moment that exhibits a human being stripped of any capacity to make either use or sense of the world. In the old man's beating on the box one sees the ultimate reduction of human expression to a kind of primitive marking — paratactic, rhythmic (or perhaps arhythmic), alogical, gestural, and non-verbal. One feels there is really no coherence here at all, no mind, no shaping spirit, yet the process of reduction does not stop at this point. In the poem's final image we see the old man returned to a merely physical presence. For at last he has fallen asleep, and so sinks down into the physical basis of life, the matrix of nature in which selfhood is completely dissolved. The poem is a kind of opposite to the first one we examined in this chapter, "Beech," a perigee to its apogee. He "keeps" the countryside, but only in an ironic sense: he is rather kept by it, and at last he seems to become an example of the complete absorption of the human by nature. We know, of course, that he is not dead, for he shifts once in his sleep. He is, however, a bit like a hibernating animal. This comparison might remind one of the conclusion of "After Apple-Picking," yet here there is no realization, no accomplishment, no Keatsian harvest of experience. There is only the night, and those three things that haunt the passages of Frost's imagination: darkness and snow and the idea of the complete expunging of any human presence.

Conclusion

We find in the selection of Frost's work that we have looked at in this chapter a simultaneous sense of human capacity and limit, of the power to construct and shape a world with a sense of the inherent limits of this power. There is the almost imperious capacity of mind, a kind of sovereignty, which we find in the first piece we looked at, "Beech," then a circumspect and alert awareness — modest, precise, and conscious of its place in the overall scheme of the world — that we saw in "The Wood-Pile," and then the various instances of internal trouble we concluded with — isolation, disorientation, even disintegration. Is it possible to answer now the questions that we started with? Taken together these questions are concerned with the basic issue of whether human existence can be said to be "worth it" or not.

There is perhaps a radical ambiguity in Frost's work on this very point. It does not seem to me that any one reader, drawing evidence from a disparate and diverse body of work, itself the product of 60 years of writing, can really resolve this ambiguity. I personally sense what I would have to describe as a gradual darkening of vision, and a feeling, arising from that, that the author might at length have been inclined to answer this question in the negative. And yet for every dark and even frightening poem, there are always more genial and affirmative ones, and, in addition, the constant presence of beauty — the habitual beauty of imagery — most of it derived from the natural world — and of style: graceful and clear as a stream of water in which these images are shown to best advantage, in which they are made manifest as though by their own natural light. Deleuze, as we have mentioned, speaks of maintaining what he called a faith in the world, and he saw the medium of film as a way of helping people to maintain such a faith. Yet faith in the world can only mean a feeling that human existence somehow *is* worth it.

Perhaps for someone to maintain this faith, two things might be needed: an outlook which is able to move beyond a narrow anthropocentrism toward a broader vision that in some way encompasses the whole of nature in all its diverse processes and, secondly, an ongoing and deeply rooted receptivity to beauty. Perhaps these are the reasons that Deleuze himself chose to focus much of his later thinking on film — the cinematic montage moves beyond the concerns of any given "I"; indeed it encompasses space and time themselves. And yet it does this through a continual and seductive appeal to the eye: a revelation of the beauty of the world, and of light itself. Perhaps there is something a bit similar going on in Frost's work, as strange as the comparison might seem at first. A possible lapse into a deep pessimism is partly averted through a perspective which gradually widens to look beyond the human (though of course it can never leave it entirely behind and would not want to) and through a continual awareness — represented in the writing itself — of beauty.

CHAPTER FIVE

World: Imagining Totality in a Post-anthropocentric Context

THE LAST MOWING

There's a place called Faraway Meadow
We never shall mow in again,
Or such is the talk at the farmhouse:
The meadow is finished with men.
Then now is the chance for the flowers
That can't stand mowers and plowers.
It must be now, though, in season
Before the not mowing brings trees on,
Before trees, seeing the opening,
March into a shadowy claim.
The trees are all I'm afraid of,
That flowers can't bloom in the shade of;
It's no more men I'm afraid of;
The meadow is done with the tame.
The place for the moment is ours
For you, O tumultuous flowers,
To go to waste and go wild in,
All shapes and colors of flowers,
I needn't call you by name.

The fact that the meadow is "finished with men" may be taken as an expression of the inessential nature of human beings, of the fact that they are not necessary to the life of the world. For curiously it is not the men who are finished with the meadow — it is not theirs to be finished with — but it which is finished with them. The assumption is that humans have no proper claim upon the world, and that by its own autonomous processes it may simply make itself unavailable to them, unavailable to their use and perhaps inhospitable to their life itself. This, then, is the overall context the poem establishes in its opening lines. With this vision as a background, the poet attempts to relate himself in some way to the world, which otherwise has become strangely remote, despite its beauty, which paradoxically perhaps is now all the more evident. He does this by means of language, of course, a calling. Yet it is a calling, and quite pointedly not even quite a naming, which is crucially informed by sight, by vision and visibility: "all shapes and colors of flowers." This attempt reduces to essentials the basic human relationship to the world: he wants merely to look, and not to use. He seeks not definite knowledge, but merely the act of seeing, of witnessing the existence of the world. Even the uniquely human capacity — the mythically Adamic capacity — of naming is given up in favor of the pure language of the eye which sees merely colors and forms. We are left with a sense of human existence cut off from the life of nature going on all around it (the flowers after all are "tumultuous," and the trees march into their shadowy claim), which it witnesses at a remove, the distance between wherever the speaker stands and Faraway Meadow. Yet the tone is not tragic; it creates the feeling of saying farewell to a relationship that perhaps was never successful in the first place. The feeling is valedictory rather than tragic.

Yet perhaps every valedictory impulse is a prelude to some attempt at imagining the totality. Are we debarred, we post-moderns, from attempting such imagination? Yet if we do make such attempts, it must be in a different way than our predecessors did. For one thing, we must try to think from two perspectives at once: our own and that of the world in itself.

Imagining the World Without Humans

DESIGN

I found a dimpled spider, fat and white,
On a white heal-all, holding up a moth
Like a white piece of rigid satin cloth —
Assorted characters of death and blight
Mixed ready to begin the morning right,
Like the ingredients of a witches' broth —
A snow-drop spider, a flower like a froth,
And dead wings carried like a paper kite. . . .

The moth is like "a white piece of rigid satin cloth," and at the end it is compared to a "paper kite." The spider is compared oddly to a snow drop to emphasize its ghastly whiteness, and the flower is deliberately stripped of any sentimental associations. Finally, the entire complex is referred to as "assorted characters of death and blight." Nature seems to have attracted the speaker's eye, and yet repelled him at the same time. There is thus a paradox inherent in the poem so far. Although nature is accessible to the senses, it is remote from our desire, and our imaginative life generally. It is perfectly possible to know it at a certain level: one merely has to observe it carefully. Yet the paradox is focused when we recognize that the closer we look, the more alien it seems. Indeed there is a strong sense of unease that animates the entire octave. Yet the exact reason for this negative tone is still unclear, and may seem somewhat exaggerated in relation to the subject.

We would expect to find the resolution of this problem in the sestet but do not. Instead we are given two rhetorical questions:

> What had that flower to do with being white,
> The wayside blue and innocent heal-all?
> What brought the kindred spider to that height,
> Then steered the white moth thither in the night?

These are followed by a third question that conceals an answer, "What but design of darkness to appall? — / If design govern in a thing so small." The answer here is, "design of darkness." Is one to take this phrase as a sufficient reason for the tone of the octave? It is actually somewhat vague, and the line that follows is a hypothetical dependent construction. Rather than explanation or clarification, the sestet seems dominated by a sense of bafflement. Its purpose would seem to be to illustrate the mind's frustration as it recognizes that none of its concepts is applicable to the object it nonetheless has so clearly before it. The poet sees but cannot understand. This inability to comprehend even seems to prompt a certain horror. It would be easy, however, to exaggerate this response or to mistake its character. Certainly there has been a tendency to place heavy emphasis on this aspect of the poem. Yet we might see the sense of horror that is frequently ascribed to it as being out of proportion to the subject — a couple of insects. And we might ask ourselves why it nonetheless remains disturbing. Is it really so frightening that spiders kill moths? Is a debunking of the old argument from design really so terrifying? What else could be the source of the poem's power?

To answer this question we must look at the octave again, particularly those phrases which seem to lead our attention in a certain direction. As we have already pointed out, the insects are characterized as "assorted characters of death and blight." This line may be somewhat heavy-handed, but it is consistent with the overall intention of making the scene appear as strange and as remote as possible. Of course, it is not remote in the sense of being distant; indeed we see it close up. It is remote rather in the sense of being impossible to assimilate to our desires, our habits, and our sentiments. That is, we cannot identify with any of the elements in this tableau, whether spider or moth — nor can we sympathize with them. By "sympathize" I mean something fairly specific but perhaps difficult to define. There is a helpful passage, however, in Richard Rorty's *Philosophy and the Mirror of Nature.* The context is a discussion of feeling, pre-linguistic awareness, and the extent to which our ability to discuss validly internal states should be viewed as an entirely social construction:

> Babies and the more attractive sorts of animals are credited with "having feelings" rather than (like photoelectric cells and animals which no one feels sentimental about — e.g., flounders and spiders) "merely responding to stimuli." This is to be explained on the basis of that sort of community feeling which unites us with anything humanoid. To be humanoid is to have a human face, and the most important part of that face is a mouth which we can imagine uttering sentences in synchrony with appropriate expressions of the face as a whole. (Rorty 189)

I do not mean to endorse Rorty's views. In fact, they seem questionable in a number of ways; yet the passage is useful for pointing out one fundamental way we *do* tend to have of relating to other natural creatures: that is, a very deeply rooted anthropocentrism which tends to extend imaginative identification to more-or-less humanoid creatures (and thus, in Rorty's view, crediting them with having feelings) while withholding it from others. Frost's choice, therefore, to represent a couple of insects is apt. The octave, with its close-up view, its meticulous description, and the feeling it has of a composed tableau gives us essentially a microcosm in which the only forms of life are ones with which we cannot really identify. The speaker of the poem is reduced to a mere observer, someone who is fundamentally excluded from what he describes. The reason is that he is peering into an alien world. In this way, we can see that the poem is ultimately about the act of thinking human beings out of the picture, and about what it is like to do this. Ultimately, it is about imagining a world which human beings are simply not a part of. In order to get the full import of this idea across to other human beings (us), he chooses to focus our attention on insects. The purpose, however, is not to scare the reader with the (presumably) horrible image of a spider killing a moth nor to debunk the theological argument from design to which the title of the poem alludes. The poem actually strikes much deeper than that, addressing the innate tendency of which such an argument is only one manifestation. The tendency is quite simply that of seeing ourselves as necessary and central to the world, rather than entirely accidental to it. "Design" is critical of some of the most ingrained habits of thought that we have. It attempts to nudge us away not only from inapplicable concepts of order but also from the anthropocentric assumptions out of which they arise.

The Fragile Thing Made Powerful

Yet these assumptions require a deeper attack still. They require that we interrogate our assumption of having a right to own and to control the world and by this means to go forth and multiply, as the phrase has it. And yet what if the pursuit of the former set of objectives — ownership and control — should end up conflicting with the latter, the continued survival of humans as a species? This is the ecological dilemma in its purest and simplest form, and it is the subject of one of Frost's most powerful though sometimes overlooked poems. In the "Census Taker," we find an account of ecological devastation vividly presented. And, interestingly, at the same time there is the perception that human beings also might disappear. The destruction of the environment and the end of human beings and human history are linked in the consciousness of a troubled narrator. We are shown that the fragility and smallness of humans, though apparently transcended by means of technology, is never really transcended, and we are shown further that the technological manipulation of nature is finally a deluded enterprise, at least insofar as it heedlessly attempts to address merely the desires of creatures who are only one part of the overall scheme of nature.

Yet we are in danger of making the poem seem more tendentious than it is. The narrator's story, his surprise and suppressed horror at finding no one at all around, and the process by which he briefly reimagines their lives and then moves outward in time and place to consider matters of archeology and pre-history, create a rich and nuanced work. As well, it is written in Frost's flexible blank verse which, though at times rather loose and free-wheeling, is in fact one of his important technical contributions to modern poetry, providing a responsive medium for the presentation of mundane realities and actual turns of speech. Here it proves useful in rendering the look and feel of a place — an area of the New England woods which has been cut for lumber. We feel very much *in situ* and as though we are given direct access to the narrator's dawning awareness. In fact, it is soon clear that a somewhat graver tone will have to combine with the conversational one.

> I came an errand one cloud-blowing evening
> To a slab-built, black-paper-covered house
> Of one room and one window and one door,
> The only dwelling in a waste cut over

A hundred square miles round it in the mountains:
And that not dwelt in now by men or women.
(It never had been dwelt in, though, by women,
So what is this I make a sorrow of?)
I came as census-taker to the waste
To count the people in it and found none,
None in the hundred miles, none in the house,
Where I came last with some hope, but not much,
After hours' overlooking from the cliffs
An emptiness flayed to the very stone.
I found no people that dared show themselves,
None not in hiding from the outward eye.

The poet begins in a straightforward manner, but after half a dozen lines he laments the absence of people, an absence which is emphasized and re-emphasized: "None . . . none . . . none." Moreover, the landscape has not just been lumbered, it has been "flayed to the very stone" and is now "an emptiness." By the end of line 16 it is clear that the speaker's errand has taken him into the midst of a complete wasteland.

In the following section the poet reinforces this sense of waste with more specific images: he tells us of a landscape totally denuded for commercial purposes. The impression is one of complete devastation; men have not merely exploited nature, they have nearly succeeded in destroying it, or at least certain aspects of it. Yet this is still merely preliminary. The heart of the poem begins at line 25, as the narrator's attention moves back from the landscape and focuses on the human dwelling in the foreground.

Perhaps the wind the more without the help
Of breathing trees said something of the time
Of year or day the way it swung a door
Forever off the latch, as if rude men
Passed in and slammed it shut each one behind him
For the next one to open for himself.
I counted nine I had no right to count
(But this was dreamy unofficial counting)
Before I made the tenth across the threshold.
Where was my supper? Where was anyone's?
No lamp was lit. Nothing was on the table.
The stove was cold — the stove was off the chimney —
And down by one side where it lacked a leg.
The people that had loudly passed the door
Were people to the ear but not the eye.
They were not on the table with their elbows.

They were not sleeping in the shelves of bunks.
I saw no men there and no bones of men there.
I armed myself against such bones as might be
With the pitch-blackened stub of an ax-handle
I picked up off the straw-dust-covered floor.
Not bones, but the ill-fitted window rattled.
The door was still because I held it shut
While I thought what to do that could be done —
About the house — about the people not there.

The narrator is nearly mesmerized by the old door banging in the wind. Yet his lapse into reverie is difficult to interpret. Is it melancholy occasioned by the sense of devastation, and thus something akin to a musing upon ruins? This might be appropriate, yet the passage does not really seem to have a negative tone. Before we can decide on this, however, he has roused himself and proceeded across the threshold. The tone at this point is remarkable: "Where was my supper? Where was anyone's?" It might almost be a type of mockery. The speaker seems deliberately brisk in dealing with these ruins; there is a conspicuous absence or avoidance of solemnity. In this way, he avoids stock responses in favor of a more truthful presentation. Yet this does not mean that he is unaffected. On the contrary, the succeeding passage registers a profound shock, yet it is of a kind that can only express itself through accurate description and shuns overt pathos. In fact, it is so great that he has to "arm himself against such bones as might be" with an old ax handle. Although this is not to be taken literally, it is to be taken seriously. Just as certain other unpleasant realities can only be approached through jokes, the reality of annihilation confronting him is so great that it forces him into this uneasy jesting. Bloom has referred to Frost's "cherubic scorn," which he relates to Emerson's cheerful and brusque disregard of sentiment and conventional piety.[1] Such scorn might indeed be present here, for it certainly is in some other Frost poems — in the flatly accurate grimness of "Out, Out" or in the derisive mockery of "The Vindictives." Yet here the joke turns around a pessimistic realization that not even Frost could be entirely comfortable with. This is brought out in the last lines in which the speaker wonders what to do "about the people not there." Here the burden of consciousness is the feeling that human life might well cease. Such fears are made more acute in the present instance, since it is so apparent that in this particular area it already has. The anxiety is greater still when we realize that human beings themselves have brought this about, for it is clear that human extinction is merely a possible result of human foolishness. This point is taken up and expanded in the concluding section:

This house in one year fallen to decay
Filled me with no less sorrow than the houses
Fallen to ruin in ten thousand years
Where Asia wedges Africa from Europe.
Nothing was left to do that I could see
Unless to find that there was no one there
And declare to the cliffs too far for echo,
"The place is desert, and let whoso lurks
In silence, if in this he is aggrieved,
Break silence now or be forever silent.
Let him say why it should not be declared so."
The melancholy of having to count souls
Where they grow fewer and fewer each year
Is extreme where they shrink to none at all.
It must be I want life to go on living.

The first four lines present us with a surprising shift in perspective. Instead of what is immediately before him, the poet speaks of what is remote. We might say that his thoughts turn archaeological. This might have been suggested by the fact that the landscape has been turned into a kind of desert, and that the human dwelling in it is in some ways the equivalent of ancient remains, the traces of a vanished presence. Clearly, he wants us to draw this comparison. Yet it is one that is not completely valid. The reason is obvious: the houses he refers to lasted ten thousand years, whereas this one before him lasted only one. We might sometimes feel that Frost's imagination is rooted entirely in his own time and place; in comparison to his modernist colleagues, he is not generally concerned with attempting to imagine the history or origin of our culture. Yet here he clearly entertains an idea of human origins in his thoughts of "the houses / Fallen to ruin in ten thousand years / Where Asia wedges Africa from Europe." It is there that nature inexplicably brought forth a new development, a new dimension within itself, that of the human: and it is therefore the source of the coexistence of these dimensions, of the confluence of these two streams — the human and the natural — and the hypothetical starting point of their difficult coexistence.

It is a difficult coexistence perhaps, but not impossible, for the houses did last ten thousand years. Surely there must have been something fundamentally right about the life carried on in that place, as opposed to the ravagement which he sees in front of him. Surely what lasted ten thousand years was more wisely attuned to its natural context, which was a desert to begin with, than this which lasted only one year and left a desert after it. Perhaps there is a certain irony implicit in the formal language of that apostrophe he makes to the surrounding cliffs, as though, in using a slightly self-conscious bravado he wanted to try to lessen the seriousness of his actual preoccupations, in order not to seem pretentious; but this cannot disguise the speaker's deep concern. Indeed, he is moved to the point of confession. Yet the melancholy that afflicts him in the last lines is occasioned by the actual possibility that human life might cease. It is made more acute, furthermore, and given greater depth, by his feeling that the relation of humans to the natural world has been perverted and is in fact approaching a crisis. It is this sense of things in crisis that motivates the poem. There is an irony, therefore, in the sense that the technological capacities which give human beings — small, essentially fragile creatures — such power over nature result in their own possible extinction. This is not an immediate danger, of course; but the poem borders on a prophetic mode unusual for this writer (one suspects he might have been somewhat uneasy with it), and so he casts ahead in his imagination, assessing what the future might bring about on the basis of what he sees before him.

Thus "The Census Taker" addresses the exploitation of the natural environment through an unwise and arrogant presumption. It is this gross calculation of ways and means, oblivious of quality or nuance — a vulgar pragmatism we may call it — which the poem criticizes, and in doing so it probably comes as close to locating the essential error of American civilization as any single short work by a modern writer. Yet besides diagnosing the cause, it goes further and makes a prognosis by foreseeing the ultimate result of this error. What is more remarkable is that the poet accomplishes this without recourse to apocalyptic rhetoric, but through mere description. In this his avoidance of the conventions of elegy and apocalyptic, combined with his usual rhetorical constraint, allows him to reveal the full significance of actual fact, and, without exaggeration, to speak fully and movingly to his subject, one with which we are now quite familiar and which we would refer to as the fate of the earth.

Dwelling and Beyond the Human

> . . . es sind
> noch Lieder zu singen jenseits
> der Menschen.
>
> — "Fadensonnen," Paul Celan

If the plight of the world is real, then perhaps we should endeavor to change our culture radically. "The Census Taker" and "Design" in a sense seek to cure us of the illusion that we are central to the world and have some right to control it, or even the ability to do so. They ask that instead we recognize the radical otherness of things, and their radical destiny beyond our uses and desires. With "Directive" this recognition comes with a new note of finality, and so it is the most grave and chastening of Frost's poems.[2]

The opening is certainly one of the most rhetorical passages he ever wrote, and its comparative formality creates a somewhat hieratic tone. We are being introduced to realities beyond our ordinary experience and therefore need the direction of someone of greater knowledge and insight. Thus, the poet declares himself our guide and leads us "out of all this now too much for us" and backward in time to some supposed source or hallowed ground. Yet the place we are directed to is notable for its absences: the house, the farm, the town are all "no more." In fact, the comparison is to graveyard sculpture which has had its details "burned, dissolved, and broken off." Apparently we are to enjoy an apprehension cleansed of such obstructive particulars. Yet what sort of conception is it in which houses, farms, and towns count as mere details? Our attention has been arrested by an overt rhetoric wielded by someone claiming to be our guide. By this means we have been lured away from everyday concerns and conducted through a sequence of emphatic negations. Yet now, what are we left with? The answer, of course, can only come through the gradual process of revelation that is the body of the poem. The first impression we have is of nature reclaiming a once-populated area. Yet the view of nature in the following lines is different from that of most Romantic poems:

> The road there, if you'll let a guide direct you
> Who only has at heart your getting lost,
> May seem as if it should have been a quarry —
> Great monolithic knees the former town
> Long since gave up pretense of keeping covered.
> And there's a story in a book about it:
> Besides the wear of iron wagon wheels
> The ledges show lines ruled southeast-northwest,
> The chisel work of an enormous Glacier
> That braced his feet against the Arctic Pole.
> You must not mind a certain coolness from him
> Still said to haunt this side of Panther Mountain.

It is true that the passage suggests some kind of spirit of place, aboriginal and vaguely hostile. Yet the details and figures seem chosen to emphasize not the hostility but the alien character, the strangeness of something fundamentally unrelated to human existence and incommensurable with human thought. This is the case despite a certain anthropomorphizing of the landscape which, it seems to me, is done only to make the place more strange, not more familiar. In fact, the details (the "monolithic knees," the glacier doing its chisel work) seem deliberately contrived, intended not to convince but to illustrate their own artificiality in order to show how attempts to domesticate the landscape's otherness are delusory. That this sense of strangeness be maintained is crucial, since as the passage continues, we realize that the journey is gradually becoming a rite of passage for us the readers precisely in our capacity as readers, a capacity which includes (and perhaps implies) our fundamental alienation from this landscape. As we make our way along, watched all the time from haunted cellar holes and rustling woods, we may sense, perhaps uneasily, that the poet is somehow watching us and, as it were, testing us in some way. As with some poems by Whitman, "Crossing Brooklyn Ferry," for example, the poet himself becomes a ghostly attendant on the very process of our reading. Frost has few parallels with Whitman, yet this is an unusual poem for Frost, and we do feel that he seeks some kind of intimacy with the reader. Yet, unlike Whitman, he complicates this process by a somewhat confrontational posture: he seems to be at once taking our measure and mocking us; informing and describing, yet all the while maintaining a contemptuous coldness — questioning, riddling, and obscurely accusatory:

> Make yourself up a cheering song of how
> Someone's road home from work this once was,
> Who may be just ahead of you on foot
> Or creaking with a buggy load of grain.
> The height of the adventure is the height
> Of country where two village cultures faded
> Into each other. Both of them are lost.
> And if you're lost enough to find yourself
> By now, pull in your ladder road behind you
> And put a sign up CLOSED to all but me.

Not only does he place a landscape before us and conduct us through it, but he also insinuates himself into our awareness. We become increasingly conscious of his vigilance, his austere and somewhat judicative role. If the landscape is the text presented to the mind's eye, then the poet's voice is the sub-text presented to the ear, an audible presence that seeks to become an ethical one. Yet this is not necessarily a gentle, or genteel, process, and we must not be surprised at the note of mockery that haunts the poem. There is a bitter irony in the phrase "Make yourself up a cheering song," which effectively mocks our attempts to evade the fact of mortality. The following two lines augment this irony with a ghostly evocation of the long-dead laborer "Who may be just ahead of you on foot / Or creaking with a buggy load of grain." The effect is haunting and conveys an unusual feeling, something beyond mere irony or mere elegy but a difficult and humanly remote combination of both, as though the poet were as contemptuous of what he memorializes as he is moved by it. The tone continues in the next lines as we are led on further toward the "height of the adventure" which turns out to be no more than the place where two villages once were. Surely now the point of the whole journey will be revealed. Yet the revelation is entirely anticlimactic, if it can be said to come at all. For all we are shown is the flat and final reality of human annihilation.

Having come to the halfway point of the poem we have been led to the presumed source and have been shown that there is nothing there. Yet the poet has to give us time to absorb the meaning of this. Actually, it is part of his intention that we should not be able to absorb it right away, that we should in fact be somewhat disoriented, for he makes it clear that only by being shaken out of our normal composure can we hope to gain anything from his instruction: "And if you're lost enough to find yourself / By now, pull in your ladder road behind you / And put a sign up CLOSED to all but me." It is a conditional arrangement: only those capable of being moved to unease and wonder will have a chance of understanding. Others, the "wrong ones" he speaks of at the end, are pointedly excluded. Thus, in the poem's climactic section, it is only to this elect group that he offers his final eloquence:

> First there's the children's house of make-believe,
> Some shattered dishes underneath a pine,
> The playthings in the playhouse of the children.
> Weep for what little things could make them glad.
> Then for the house that is no more a house,
> But only a belilaced cellar hole,
> Now slowly closing like a dent in dough.
> This was no playhouse but a house in earnest.

Certainly these are among the most moving lines Frost ever wrote. We are shown the remnants of human lives as though they were relics. But what are they really? Nothing but broken dishes and a hole in the ground. The passage moves between these two perspectives: the memorializing and the reductive. In this way it expresses an ambivalence which is at the heart of the poem as a whole. On the one hand, elegiac pathos:

"Weep for what little things could make them glad"; and on the other, withering irony: "This was no playhouse but a house in earnest." We notice, however, that the last word is given to the voice of irony and to its terrible vision of extinction. It is as if this last of human sentiments — elegiac memory and reverence for the dead — is being subjected to a violent reduction. We begin to see that the entire poem has been a kind of leveling process directed at human presumption, for by now, despite its indirections, its moral tenor is clear. It seeks to deny a privileged status to human beings, whether that status be based on the idea that humans possess reason or even on the fact that they are uniquely aware of their own mortality. In this view human beings are not central to the world but transient creatures in it of no special significance, and any pretense otherwise is an illusion which must be dispelled.

This is not to say that elegiac sentiments are wrong, for only by going through such emotions can one move beyond them. Yet it is necessary to move beyond them if one is to achieve the final clarity that the poet holds out to us at the end of the poem, the completely disabused sobriety which he calls being "beyond confusion." In those concluding lines a sobering draught is offered to us, yet we can take it only if we manage to move beyond what Pater called the "pitiful awe and care for the perishing human clay"(131). Such a directive might seem extreme or unreasonable, and in a sense it is both. The poem seeks such extremity; it seeks to push us beyond our normal concerns so that we recognize our true condition. Yet the sane and sacred nihilism which descends on the poet in this final passage is not for everyone, as he himself tells us, for not everyone could understand its proper significance. Such people are the "wrong ones" who must not get saved, must not acquire such knowledge. In their hands it would degenerate into the facile and violent nihilism with which we are familiar. By contrast Frost introduces us to what we might call a poised nihilism. It is poised in that it does not seek to overturn anything; it has no iconoclastic element, no affinity with violence. It does not come as a Dionysian outbreak but as a sobering influence which dissolves the illusions of anthropocentrism. In "Directive" the idea of human beings as owners, stewards, or central figures in the landscape is destroyed. We are conducted to a source that is not a source but merely the place that shows us most clearly our fundamental poverty. It is to this that we must be periodically returned and so brought to recognize the terms of our actual condition in the world.

The idea of origins is a theme that emerges from time to time in Frost. We see it in the eddy whorl of "West Running Brook," in the hypothetical place of human origins spoken of in "The Census Taker"

("Where Asia wedges Africa from Europe"), and finally in the cold spring of "Directive." Yet the idea of an historical continuum makes possible the idea of error, of a wandering away from some initial wisdom. The ruined cabin and denuded landscape of "The Census Taker" fill the poet with melancholy, because they indicate a way of life fundamentally out of harmony with its natural context. The idea of an historically remote origin, whatever scientific validity it may have, is therefore useful since it makes possible the idea of historically augmented error, a twisting awry or perversion of human life itself.

Such an idea may have a therapeutic function for us by shocking us out of our complacent assumption that the way of life we have evolved is natural and inevitable. If the history of the species is one of compounded error, then individuals must somehow be restored to sanity. "Directive" is such an attempt, yet the source to which it directs us is not anything we might touch or have communion with. On the contrary, it attempts to pour cold water on the idea of such personal and transcendental moments. Its hieratic tone is a kind of Socratic ruse designed to show the foolishness of such self-flattering and self-deceptive transcendentalizing impulses. Far from encouraging an ahistorical moment of redemptive vision, it weighs the cost of that particular aspect of western history embodied in the idea that human beings should control nature. In this sense the poem is a moral criticism of our culturally determined anthropocentrism. It recognizes the proximity of human culture and nature yet also their irreducible difference. Because of this difference, the actions we take toward nature may not be suited to it and may indeed be destructive and their motivations fundamentally deluded. The poem, in a sense, satirizes this condition. Its ultimate purpose, however, is neither to satirize nor to provide the moment of redemptive vision other critics have seen in it but to return us to a recognition of our place in the world and of the limits of mortality.

One question we might consider more frequently, therefore, is the degree to which Frost's work can be located within a humanistic frame of reference and to what extent it tends to push beyond such a context. It is often assumed that however pessimistic his poetry may sometimes be, it nonetheless assumes the fundamental importance of human beings and their desires, values, and culture. It seems to me that though a portion of his work can be viewed in this way (and perhaps most of it can), there is still a significant part that cannot. In some of his poetry he seems to be moving entirely beyond the bounds of humanism, however broadly or loosely defined. Indeed, for my purposes here it is best to define it quite loosely as the assumption that human beings are somehow central to the world. This is the difference between the Frost of

"Directive" and most of his precursors, both immediate and remote, a crucial difference, though not absolute and not to be exaggerated, which has to do with how one thinks of human existence itself and its possibilities and limits.

The World/The Totality

Is there, then, a way to imagine the totality in a non-anthropocentric context? So far we have established the author's willingness to entertain the idea that humans are inessential to the world and perhaps should be viewed as a kind of disturbance to its order and harmony, an ancient Stoic idea come back again in a somewhat ecological guise.

The Counter-current

"West-Running Brook" begins as a dialogue between husband and wife. And it is in this section, strangely, that most of its weaknesses are apparent, I say strangely because certainly the author has given ample proof at other times of his ability to create complex characters and interesting dialogue. Here, however, it is as if his attention is not focused primarily on the pair in question but more on the abstract issues he wants them to broach. The result is a genre distantly related to the eclogue, with its bucolic setting and its dialogue serving as a pretense for a quasi-philosophical discussion (though in this case it is more a monologue). We might consider briefly, however, despite the relative lameness of the dialogue, what the purpose could be of having husband and wife, man and woman, both participate equally in what is essentially a discussion of metaphysics, ontology, and cosmology. In Luce Irigaray, for example, we are shown that it is not possible for the sexes to arrive at their respective and complete intellectual attainments independently of each other. The theme of the strangely titled book *I Love to You* is, among other things, this interdependence of the male and female minds which are in fact distinct and must be so in their respective orientations toward the truths of existence, truths which they instantiate in their bodies in different ways.[3] The traditional view of abstract theoretical knowledge as somehow transcending its bodily context is an illusion fostered by a patriarchal social organization and its attendant ideology. It is interesting, therefore, in this poem, which could conceivably have been written in some other format, some other genre with only the male voice speaking in a vatic and visionary way perhaps slightly reminiscent of Victor Hugo or Whitman, that at various points the author nonetheless chooses to include the woman, thus making the introductory section not merely a scene-setter but an instance, however imperfect, that the ultimate insights into the nature of the world can only come about in dialogic fashion and with both male and female voices present and participating, though admittedly it is the male voice which comes to dominate the poem's central and most significant section.

There is an initial attempt at orientation in space: "Fred, where is north?" / "North? North is there my love." The long description of the brook follows, which does not exclude an element of banter and teasing. And yet the significance of the brook's peculiar directional disposition and the fact that a wave appears to be "waving" is broached by the woman in a strange and remarkable allusion to Catholic mythology : "an annunciation," as she calls it. The annunciation was, of course, a message or a sign given by an angel to Mary. There is no specific message here, nor is any room made for a supernatural realm anywhere in the poem. Yet the idea of a sign given by nature to human beings begins the process of visionary meditation that is the poem's main achievement. Revelation here, in fact, proceeds in stages, as it usually does. There is the initial noticing: *this has happened*; or, in this case, *this is.* And then there are the layers of interpretation built upon that, in a continual attempt to extend the significance of the remarkable event without losing sight of it, without forgetting the initial moment beneath the subsequent moments of imaginative projection, interpretation, and commentary.

In a way, the poem gives us a miniature history of the process of civilization, for there is no founding or seminal body of thought, imagination, or ethical concern which does not start with precisely this — a noticing, which is then communicated to a small number of others, initiates, and which then becomes the basis of various layers of interpretive abstraction and commentary, explanation, and visionary ardor. The strata of cultural history are revealed in the layers of the poem's central monologue — a piece of visionary naturalism reminiscent in some ways of Lucretius. The seemingly naive question "Where is north?" means in effect "where are we" and "where are things" and "where are we in relation to things, the things of the world?" It is then she who uses the charged and numinous word "annunciation," a word which, given the poem's overall naturalism, must be placed in *italics*, as it were, through an irony directed her way by her husband. It is a gentle irony, certainly, though one which rings strangely to our ears these days, "tak[ing] it off to lady land." And yet though the religious overtones have been dispersed by this brief and rather lame joke, the idea itself has not — that there are natural processes which speak to all, whether they be men or women, or indeed whether they inhabit one or the other side of that major north American cultural divide which even these days is not always recognized as such — that between Catholic and Protestant. For the Catholic tradition is certainly implicit in this annunciation to a woman. And yet the Protestant tradition too had sought revelations, albeit not in mysterious announcements vouchsafed to individuals but rather in natural events themselves as seen as the images and shadows of divine things. Male and female, Catholic and Protestant, and indeed esoteric and exoteric, are balanced, if not reconciled, in the initial scene-setting of this piece, which will turn out to be the author's most visionary and oracular, the one in which he attempts to discourse *de rerum natura.* Yet this vision cannot be confined within a given cultural milieu, nor to a single gender, for it is a vision which attempts to answer the basic question — basic to all culture — of the relationship of humans to the world by first imagining the nature of the world in itself.

The central portion of the poem certainly is the most poetically significant. It presents a vision of flux of a more or less Bergsonian or Whiteheadean kind. Yet it includes the interesting detail of the eddy whorl itself, a principle of contrariness within the overall stream of time that the poem's cosmology puts forward as the essential reality of nature. The novelty of the concept lies in this idea — neither the flux nor the totality is the origin of existents. It is rather this counter-current, this counter principle, which is. Lucretius had proposed a swerving of atoms, yet here, in fact, this idea is specifically rejected. Rather than a swerving, there is a throwing back of the flux of existence upon itself not in the form of memory but in the form of some other and unspecified resistance, some sort of *connatus.* It is this that individual existents "are from":

> "The universal cataract of death
> That spends to nothingness — and unresisted,
> Save by some strange resistance in itself,
> Not just a swerving, but a throwing back,
> As if regret were in it and were sacred.
> It has this throwing backward on itself
> So that the fall of most of it is always
> Raising a little, sending up a little.
> Our life runs down in sending up the clock.
> The brook runs down in sending up our life.
> The sun runs down in sending up the brook.
> And there is something sending up the sun.
> It is this backward motion from the source,
> Against the stream, that most we see ourselves in,

The tribute of the current to the source.
It is from this in nature we are from.
It is most us."

And yet there is an interesting detail here that is, in a way, a contradiction. For if part runs down in sending up some other, smaller part, then this would mean that the smaller part would be a kind of surplus of the larger. Yet the vision of the section as a whole, and of the poems as a whole, would not seem to be that of the natural or cosmic order as continual surplus, a continual surpassing of itself — quite the opposite. It is in general a vision of process combined with the second law of thermodynamics, a vision of a universal and continual running down. These are the materials, therefore, of this rich but somewhat puzzling poem: Lucretius and his atomic swerving, invoked but somewhat refuted; Bergson and Whitehead and their vision of continual process; the basic idea of existents being surpluses "thrown up" by underlying processes, though this idea, too, is not really held to; there is as well the general idea of the second law of thermodynamics which inflects this vision of process and makes of it a universal depletion, a cataract of death; and, finally, we see even a suggestion of Levinas in the sense that Levinas proposes a god who has sunk infinitely into the past. (Perhaps he is the "something else" who is sending up the sun.)[4] Such is the rich complex of cosmological motifs informing this passage, so rich that it may not be possible to reconcile them all with each other.

We should begin with this god sunk infinitely into the past. It is because he is so that the universe takes the form the speaker attempts to describe. It is a melancholy vision, after all, a fact he repeatedly emphasizes: "It seriously, sadly, runs away." Moreover, this is a melancholy that contrasts to some extent with the overt occasion of the poem — husband and wife looking out upon the natural world. In this sense, the poem contrasts tonally to others pieces in which Frost used this same *topos* — "Two Look at Two" comes readily to mind — where an idyllic vision of nature is vouchsafed to the pair of lovers. Here, however, the substance of the revelation is one of loss and indeed universal annihilation. There is no principle which can stay this universal flux, the universal cataract of death. Not even the universe as a whole can, for the poem, in its scientific orientation, quite pointedly ignores ideas such as the recurring universe model proposed at the time by some scientists, in which the "Big Bang" would be followed by a gradual re-coalescence of the universe's dispersed matter back into its original state in a "big crunch," an oscillation which would presumably go on forever. This cosmological vision is now out of favor; physicists currently believe that there is not enough mass in the universe to cause it to re-collapse in such a way at the end of its cosmic career.[5] Rather it will continue to expand, and run down, indefinitely. This would appear to have already been Frost's vision as early as 1928, the date of the *West-Running Brook* volume. And yet if this is the fundamental principle of reality, this expenditure pure and simple, there must be some counter-principle that resists it in order for existents to be in the first place. They must exist in a universal *connatus* — the self-assertion of each and of all things. This is not a static principle, however, a mere willing to remain in existence as is. It is a dynamic one of resistance by which the universal cataract is temporarily contested. The poem creates a strangely pessimistic and at the same time remarkably dynamic vision. It is one, moreover, which complements the visions of excess, of profusion, proposed by Bataille, rendering it both bleaker and more scientific through the inclusion of the second law of thermodynamics. For no amount of energy, even that of the sun, can be viewed as unlimited in principle.

"The Pod of Milkweed": Universal Emptiness and Beauty

And yet all people and indeed all creatures live in the present. The present lives in the present, and there is nothing other than the present. It is in the present that beauty arises, and is apprehended. Thus, in implicit answer to one of our initial questions in the previous chapter — whether a profound relationship to beauty is still possible — we find "The Pod of Milkweed," which might be considered his final poem, the one which expresses his concluding vision. It is a vision of surplus, and yet of an ultimate emptiness of an almost Buddhistic kind. The creatures of the world, including human beings — for the poem wavers on the border of allegory in a sort of exquisite, neo-Spenserian fashion — are weightless, insubstantial, and yet beautiful. An over-profusion of them is brought forth, and in fact there is a certain comic element to this, a lightness of touch which complements the gravity and inherent tragedy of the vision conveyed in "West-Running Brook." At the same time, what is more fragile than a butterfly, and yet what more beautiful?

As we approach this piece, we come in some sense full circle, for at the outset, the impetus for his poetry, and for the self-dedication of the speaker to this the least recompensed of all vocations, was nothing other than the beautiful. This was, in part, beauty apprehended in the world and in part the beauty that could be felt from within — the inescapable beauty of language itself and of the forms of language bequeathed to the novice poet through the poetic tradition. Here all that is past. And the poet, led by degrees in part by a style which demanded an account of the external reality of things and the nuances of culture simultaneously, was guided through a series of stages of progressive discovery, perhaps at times of renunciation or divestiture, which included the recognition of suffering and, indeed, tragedy. And yet the presence of beauty in abundance and even over-profusion demanded to be seen, to be known; and at length it brings to his late work a vision of surplus, waste, and beauty, simultaneously. The individual existents — these butterflies — are eminently expendable, and yet there are always more of them. They are active in the sun and light, which supports their life, and yet, curiously, some seem dormant, asleep perhaps, drugged with the poppy which is their existence itself, furnished, as it must be, with manifold illusions, the illusions of pleasure, if nothing else. The *connatus* which sustains each of them against the universal cataract of death is real, and yet it is lightly borne. One has the impression that these hardly substantial creatures are brought forth by an abundance which yet is an emptiness. Their life is attended by a beauty they enjoy and are part of but which gives them, finally, nothing. Is life still possible? Human life? Is it still worth it? Was it ever? Is — and this is perhaps a deeper and more important question — is a profound relationship to beauty still possible, such that it makes existence in the world seem worthwhile? We dare to conclude our study of one of the most daring and most suggestive of poets with questions rather than answers.

Conclusion

I

Literary historians tend to be overly concerned with the idea of innovation, or with what they take to be innovation. Perhaps for this reason the historical significance of Frost's poetry has not been very well recognized. Yet its importance in the context of American literature could not be greater. The reasons for this are numerous, but one of the most important is the way it expresses some of the main impulses of American pragmatism while at the same time modifying them. Frost always attempts to dramatize the interaction between self and world, and how, in that dramatic encounter, imaginative constructs influence our actual lives. Thus, he is continually aware of the connection between thought and deed, as we might call it, between what we can imagine and what we can do, and we find in his work a mind which with the utmost discrimination continually assesses the value of any given way of conceptualizing things.[1]

Yet the crucial and distinguishing mark of Frost's pragmatism lies in his sense of the fragility of life. He was, after all, an amateur naturalist with a naturalist's feel for the delicate balances of nature. Some of this sense of inherent vulnerability comes through in his vision of human life as well. He is aware of how easy it is for people to be constrained and thwarted by their conceptions or by those which others force on them. A master of independence himself, he was always aware of how difficult it is to attain that state of balance and clarity which places one beyond violation by ideas. For ideas and the metaphors they spring from are, in his view, both tools and implements of destruction, both prescriptions and poisons.

Yet if this is true, then it must be true of the ideas of pragmatism also. Might pragmatism be merely a release from thought, a shortcut, a pernicious influence? Emerson, after all, writes *Whim* over the lintels of the door-post, hoping that it will prove better than whim at last; but he also reminds us that we cannot spend the day in explanation. Frost, it seems to me, is aware of the potential for abuse in Emerson's injunctions, for a violation of the world and of the others in it. He is aware of their potentially crude results and of how they might foster mere thoughtlessness or degenerate into the gross calculation of expediency. He is nowhere polemical on this point, and he never seeks to confront the Emersonian tradition with explicit criticism. Indeed, in the early decades of the century he is its strongest literary exponent. Nonetheless, by working with this tradition he added another dimension to it, or at least strengthened an already existing though muted element in it. He does this through an intense awareness of fragility. It may even be that the human desire which pragmatism serves, the impulse to enhance human life and enlarge the scope of human capacities, needs to be tempered and restrained. Frost seems to suggest this need for restraint in the tact and delicacy which his style everywhere exhibits and in the chastened view he has of human life itself. He continually emphasizes human finitude as well as the limits and fragility of the world. In this he is not unique among pragmatists; James and Emerson both had a strong sense of the uncertainty of human efforts. But more often they chose to project a vision of possibility. Frost, however, seems to me to distance himself from such hope. It is as if he does not expect human life to ever be very much at all. Many people have noticed this difference in tone between Frost and Emerson. But it is generally explained by the idea that Emerson believed in a Wordsworthian spirit of nature and Frost did not. The difference, however, is not so much in their vision of nature, as in their vision of the possiblities of human existence.[2]

II

At the end of his life Frost, like Wordsworth, imagined the death of nature.[3] In "The Pod of Milkweed," for example the extinction of man and the end of nature are part of the same general drift toward annihilation: clouds of butterflies, human beings, and whole worlds are equally expendable. Yet even in this poem, he shows his naturalist's love of detail and his scrupulous and reverent eye for the body of the world. Perhaps no poet has ever had a style more delicately attuned to its subject: always elegant yet wonderfully transparent, responsive to the smallest nuance of nature or of thought, attentive both to the object and to the demands of aesthetics, genre, and tradition. To speak loosely, we might say that he blends culture and nature together in his very style. In this way, he reminds us that his values of balance, clarity, and tact are not to be seen only from a human standpoint, that is, only with regard to their value and utility for human beings. Rather, he suggests that they have their full significance only when taken in the context of nature ecologically considered. Frost was not quite as solicitous of the natural environment as Thoreau, yet, as we have seen, he was acutely aware of the harm that could be done through the unrestrained pursuit of pragmatic ends. Richard Poirier refers to Frost's poetry as the work of knowing; but it is also the work of acting, of participation. The ethic which directs this process is one of attention — both to the demands of the self which must act, as well as to the body of nature, which is its ultimate context. His task is to harmonize their different claims. It is this difficult middle way that his poetry attempts to negotiate.

NOTES

INTRODUCTION

[1] The best example would be Yvor Winters's "Robert Frost: or, the Spiritual Drifter as Poet." It is the best not for its insight into Frost's poetry (it has none) but for the clear picture it gives of an intense rationalist sensibility confronted with a powerful example of pragmatism.

[2] See Keith Ansell Pearson's study *Germinal Life: The Difference and Repetition of Deleuze* for a discussion of Deleuze's connection to biological science.

[3] Deleuze's ideas on film are found in *Cinema I* and *Cinema II*; the interpretation of Spinoza I refer to is found in *Spinoza: Practical Philosophy.*

INTRODUCTION TO PART ONE

[1] This is one of the main theses of Levinas's *Time and the Other.*

CHAPTER ONE

[1] I am indebted to Richard Poirier's discussion of Rossetti in connection with Frost. See *Robert Frost: The Work of Knowing*, 32-37.

[2] I echo the introductory remarks to Rossetti in the anthology *Victorian Prose and Poetry*, eds. Harold Bloom and Lionel Trilling (New York: Oxford University Press, 1973), 615-16.

[3] See for example Gaston Bachelard's *The Poetics of Reverie*, 173-82.

[4] I am indebted to Poirier's discussion of "Waiting" in *The Work of Knowing* (65-66) for some of the basic terms of my discussion.

[5] *Robert Frost: The Work of Knowing*, 212-13. Poirier discusses the artful construction of the volume as a whole as well (28-49). For other discussions of the deliberately "made" character of the volume see Donald T. Haynes, "The Narrative Unity of A Boy's Will," 452-64; and Lewis H. Miller, Jr., "Design and Drama in *A Boy's Will*," in *Robert Frost: Centennial Essays*, ed. Jac Tharpe 351-368. For a good discussion of "Rose Pogonias" see Frank Lentricchia, *Robert Frost: Modern Poetics and the Landscapes of the Self*, 32-34.

[6] For a discussion of Valéry's "art of number" and its relation to poetry see Geoffrey Hartman, "Valéry's Fable of the Bee" in *The Fate of Reading*, 223-47.

[7] Geoffrey H. Hartman, *Wordsworth's Poetry 1787-1814*, 3-12. For a previous application of Hartman's idea of "surmise" to Frost see David L. Miller, "Dominion of the Eye in Frost."

[8] John Keats, Letter to Benjamin Bailey, Saturday 22 Nov. 1817, in *Selected Letters*, 52.

[9] See *Totality and Infinity*, in particular the section "Separation and Discourse," 53-81.

[10] See Poirier for a brilliant reading of this poem, *The Work of Knowing*, xiv-xvi.

[11] See *Totality and Infinity*, in particular the section "Enjoyment and Representation," 122-42.

[12] Paul Valéry, "Palme." In *Paul Valéry: An Anthology*, 278-84.

CHAPTER TWO

[1] See Keith Ansell Pearson, *Germinal Life*, 124.

[2] Badiou, *The Clamor of Being*, passim.

[3] John Keats, Letter to George and Thomas Keats, Sunday 21 Dec. 1817, *Selected Letters* 55. See also the discussion of Negative Capability in Walter Jackson Bates's *Keats*, 5.

[4] See D. W. Winnicott, "The Development of the Capacity for Concern" in *The Maturational Process*, and "The Location of Cultural Experience" in *Playing and Reality*. For an investigation of the relationship between Keatsian Negative Capability and Winnicott's psychoanalytic theories see Brooke Hopkins, "Keats' Negative Capability and Winnicott's Creative Play" *American Imago* 41 (1984): 85-100. Hopkins argues that Negative Capability should be seen as neither passive nor active in the conventional sense but part of a condition that "according to Winnicott makes true play and hence creativity possible. . . . " This creativity is then seen as, in Winnicott's terms, part of the fundamental "capacity to be" which is necessary to the "perpetual human task of keeping inner and outer reality separate yet interrelated . . . " (Winnicott, *Playing and Reality* 65). For a discussion of the relation of Winnicott's ideas of play and creativity to the general context of American Pragmatism see Richard Poirier's "Frost, Burke, Winnicott."

[5] See the chapters "Transgression" and "Murder, Hunting, and War," 63-80.

CHAPTER THREE

[1] See Kenneth Burke, "I, Eye, Aye — Concerning Emerson's Early Essay on 'Nature,' and the Machinery of Transcendence" in *Language as Symbolic Gesture*.

[2] For a sense of the theological and psychological ramifications of the idea of enthusiasm and the precautions taken against it see Perry Miller, *The New England Mind: The Seventeenth Century*, in particular the chapters "The Means of Conversion" and "Rhetoric." For a description and analysis of the character of some of the later revivals in the early nineteenth century, see Perry Miller, *The Life of the Mind in America*, chapter one, "The Intellect of the Revival." See also Geoffrey H. Hartman's discussion of enthusiasm in the context of Christopher Smart's "Jubilato Agno" in "Christopher Smart's Magnificat," *The Fate of Reading*, 74-98.

[3] See Sharon Cameron's *Lyric Time* for a discussion of somewhat analogous tendencies in Dickinson. She writes: "For while the most profound estrangement is that precipitated by death, in Dickinson's poems death is not loss for the dying person but is rather reunion. So at least is the poems' premise: life must be sacrificed, selfhood go by the way, all defining characteristics dismissed, but the recompense for these exactions is the end of the solitary self, the loss of the boundary between self and object, not because they are dead to each other but rather because they are fused with each other" (136-37). And further: "In the

words of another, older text, when St. Paul in the Letter to Romans (7:24) asks 'Who shall deliver me from the body of this death?' the terms of deliverance seem also to be the loss of the body if that loss could be followed by a higher union. It is in the service of union that the displacements in Dickinson's poems unfold: the 'failed Windows,' the 'Gazing Grain—,' —all the[se]projective fusions . . . are symptoms or manifestations of the desire to be one with the object of one's longing. Thus displacement itself must be regarded as a phenomenon devised to counter those boundaries that impose the intolerable distinction, and Romanticism, so obsessed with the point at which relationship becomes fusion because it cannot help it (or because it does not wish to help it), must recognize its desires, pushed to the extreme, in that longing for death which will deliver it to coincidence" (137). Frost, not nearly so Romantic as Dickinson, does not hold out any hope that death will bring about union with the object. But the process, as we see it in "To Earthward," by which the self must be surpassed in order to encounter the other, or at least attempt to, is somewhat similar.

4 I am indebted in my general reading of these two poems of Keats to the following: Earl Wasserman, *The Finer Tone*; Harold Bloom, *The Visionary Company: A Reading of English Romantic Poetry* (New York: Doubleday & Co., 1961); and Helen Vendler, *The Odes of John Keats,* particularly chapters III and VII passim. See also Richard Poirier's complex reading of "After Apple-Picking" in *The Work of Knowing,* 291-99. Other readings I have found useful include John J. Condon, "'After Apple-Picking': Frost's Troubled Sleep"; Marion Montgomery, "Robert Frost: One Who Shrewdly Pretends"; and the masterful essay by Robert Penn Warren in *Selected Essays.*

CHAPTER FOUR

1 The term "witness tree" originates in the science of surveying — i.e., a tree used to mark a boundary.

2 See Levinas's *Existence and Existents,* 21-36 and 65-101.

3 See Eben Bass. "Frost's Poetry of Fear"; and Mildred E. Hartstock, "Robert Frost: Poet of Risk."

CHAPTER FIVE

1 In the Introduction to *Modern Critical Views: Robert Frost,* Harold Bloom, ed.

2 A number of critics have considered the tone and ceremonial quality of the poem to be mere empty gestures and mannerisms. See for example, Marie Borroff, *Language and the Poet,* 40-41; a very harsh judgment on this score is made by Richard Poirier, *The Work of Knowing,* 99-100. "Directive" has been one of Frost's most widely debated poems. Some representative readings include: Robert Peters, "The Truth of Frost's 'Directive'"; William H. Pritchard, "Diminished Nature," *Massachusetts Review* 1 (May 1960): 475-92; S.P.C. Duvall, "Robert Frost's 'Directive' Out of Walden"; Margaret M. Blum, "Robert Frost's 'Directive': A Theological Reading"; George Knox, "A Backward Motion Toward the Source"; J. P. Dougherty, "Robert Frost's 'Directive' to the Wilderness"; Reuben Brower, *The Poetry of Robert Frost,* 226-42; Frank Lentricchia, *Robert Frost,* 112-19

3 Irigaray, *I Love to You*, chapter one and passim.

4 See Levinas's *Otherwise than Being*, in particular chapter five.

5 Alphonso Lingis has produced this remarkable summary:

> The astrophysicists Fred Adams and Greg Laughlin have constructed the hitherto most complete scientific analysis of the fate of the universe. The received astrophysical wisdom today is that there is not quite enough gravitational force exerted by all the matter in the universe to cause it to recollapse in a Big Crunch after sixty or a hundred billion years. Adams and Laughlin have projected the future of the universe to the next two hundred cosmological decades — a cosmological decade being one-followed-by-two-hundred-zeroes years. We are currently midway through this era. It will come to an end when all the stars burn out. Our sun, four and a half billion years old, is half-way to burning itself out. It will eventually puff up into a red giant and then collapse into a white dwarf no bigger than the Earth. In the process the sun will broil away earth's oceans, leaving an uninhabitable cinder, which will perhaps spiral into the sun.
>
> The next era the astrophysicists name the Degenerate Era. The mass of the cosmos will be locked up in the dim, dense hulks of failed, dead, exploded, and collapsed stars — white dwarfs, brown dwarfs, neutron stars, and black holes. Galaxies will begin to fall apart. As the degenerate hulks collide or sweep close to each other, some will move out beyond the fringes and go careening through intergalactic space, while others will fall toward the galactic centers. . . .
>
> Toward the end of this epoch, about one hundred trillion trillion trillion years from now, the protons in the heart of every atom will begin to decay. The remaining white dwarfs and neutron stars will dissipate, converting a large fraction of the ordinary mass in the cosmos to radiation and ending the Degenerate Era. The final, Dark Era will consist in a diffuse sea of electrons, positrons, neutrinos, and radiation spread tenuously across an enormously larger region than exists today.
>
> (*Dangerous Emotions* 135-36)

CONCLUSION

1 Mark Richardson presents able discussions of how this conceptualizing and reconceptualizing works in Frost's poetry as well as in his sense of vocation. See *The Ordeal of Robert Frost*, especially his discussion of the poem "Good Hours" (69-79).

2 For a discussion of whether pragmatism has been a positive or negative influence on American intellectual life, see Richard Rorty, "Pragmatism, Relativism, Irrationalism" in *Consequences of Pragmatism*, 160-75.

3 See Geoffrey H. Hartman, *Wordsworth's Poetry 1787-1814* (333-38).

WORKS CITED

Ammons, A.R. *Corsons Inlet.* Ithaca: Cornell University Press, 1965.

Bachelard, Gaston. The *Poetics of Reverie.* Trans. Daniel Russell. New York: Orion Press, 1969.

Badiou, Alain. *Deleuze: The Clamor of Being.* Trans. Louise Burchill. Minneapolis: University of Minnesota Press, 2000.

Bass, Eben. "Frost's Poetry of Fear." *American Literature* 43 (Jan. 1972): 603-15.

Bataille, Georges. *The Accursed Share: An Essay on General Economy.* Trans. Robert Hurley. New York: Zone Books, 1988.

———. *Erotism.* Trans. Mary Dalwood. San Francisco: City Lights, 1986.

Bate, Walter Jackson. *John Keats.* Cambridge: Belknap Press of Harvard University Press, 1963.

Berger, Charles. "Echoing Eden: Frost and Origins." *Modem Critical Views: Robert Frost.* Ed. Harold Bloom. New York: Chelsea House Publishers, 1986. 147-65.

Blackmur, R.P. "The Instincts of a Bard" (Review Essay). *The Nation* 142 (June 24, 1936): 817-19.

Bloom, Harold. Introduction. *Modern Critical Views: Robert Frost.* Ed. Harold Bloom. New York: Chelsea House Publishers, 1986. 1-7.

Bloom, Harold and Lionel Trilling, eds. *Victorian Prose and Poetry:* New York: Oxford University Press, 1973.

Blum, Margaret M. "Robert Frost's 'Directive': A Theological Reading." *Modem Language Notes* 76 (June): 524-25.

Borroff, Marie. "Robert Frost's New Testament: The Uses of Simplicity." *Language and the Poet: Verbal Artistry in Frost, Stevens, and Moore.* Chicago: University of Chicago Press, 1979.

———. "Robert Frost: 'To Earthward.'" *Robert Frost: Centennial Essays II.* Ed. Jac Tharpe. Jackson: University of Mississippi Press, 1976.

Brower, Reuben. *The Poetry of Robert Frost: Constellations of Intention.* New York: Oxford University Press, 1963.

Burke, Kenneth. *Language as Symbolic Gesture.* Berkeley: University of California Press, 1966.

Cameron, Sharon. *Lyric Time: Dickinson and the Limits of Genre.* Baltimore and London: The Johns Hopkins University Press, 1979.

Celan, Paul. *Paul Celan: Poems.* Translated and selected by Michael Hamburger. Manchester: Carcanet New Press, 1980.

Condon, John J. "'After Apple-Picking': Frost's Troubled Sleep." *Robert Frost Centennial Essays.* Ed. Jac Tharpe. Jackson: University of Mississippi Press, 1974. 171-81.

Cook, Reginald L. "The Critics and Robert Frost." In *Robert Frost: Centennial Essays.* Ed. Jac Tharpe. University of Mississippi Press: Jackson, 1974. 15-30.

Deleuze, Gilles. *The Logic of Sense*. Trans. Mark Lester with Charles Stivale. London: Athlone Press, 1990.

———. *Difference and Repetition*. Trans. Paul Patton. London: Athlone Press, 1994.

———. *Cinema I: Movement-Image*. Trans. Hugh Tomlinson and Barbara Habberjam. London: Athlone Press, 1986.

———. *Cinema II: Time-Image*. Trans. Hugh Tomlinson and Robert Galeta. London: Athlone Press, 1989.

———. *Spinoza: Practical Philosophy* . Trans. Robert Hurley. San Francisco: City Lights, 1988.

Deleuze, Gilles and Felix Guattari. *Anti-Oedipus: Capitalism and Schizophrenia*. Trans. R. Hurley, M. Seem, H. R. Lane. London: Athlone Press, 1984.

Dougherty, James P. "Robert Frost's 'Directive' to the Wilderness." *American Quarterly* 18 (Summer 1966): 209-19.

Duvall, S.P.C. "Robert Frost's 'Directive' Out of Walden." *American Literature* 31 (Jan 1960): 482-88.

Emerson, Ralph Waldo. *Essay and Lectures*. Ed. Joel Porte. New York: The Library of America, 1883.

Frost, Robert. *The Poetry of Robert Frost*. Ed. Edward Connery Lathem. New York: Henry Holt and Co., 1969.

———. *Selected Prose of Robert Frost*. Ed. Hyde Cox and Edward Connery Lathem. New York: Henry Holt and Co., 1966.

Garber, Frederick. *Thoreau's Redemptive Imagination*. New York: New York University Press, 1977.

Hartman, Geoffrey H. *The Fate of Reading*. Chicago: University of Chicago Press, 1975.

———. *The Unmediated Vision*. New Haven: Yale University Press, 1954.

———. *Wordsworth's Poetry 1787-1814*. New Haven: Yale University Press, 1964.

Hartstock, Mildred E. "Robert Frost: Poet of Risk." *Personalist* 45 (April 1964): 157-75.

Hass, Lawrence and Dorothea Olkowski, Eds. *Rereading Merleau-Ponty*. Amherst, New York: Humanity Books, 2000.

Haynes, Donald T. "The Narrative Unity of *A Boy's Will*." *PMLA* 87 (May 1972): 452-64.

Irigaray, Luce. *I Love to You: Sketch of a Possible Felicity in History*. Trans. Alison Martin. New York and London: Routledge, 1996.

Keats, John. *Complete Poems*. Ed. Jack Stillinger. Cambridge: The Belknap Press of Harvard University Press, 1982.

———. *Selected Letters*. Ed. Robert Pack. New York: New American Library, 1974.

Knox, George, "A Backward Motion Toward the Source," *Personalist* 47 (1966): 365-81.

Laing, R.D. *The Divided Self*. New York: Pantheon, 1960.

Lentricchia, Frank. *Robert Frost: Modern Poetics and the Landscapes of the Self*. Durham, N.C.: Duke University Press, 1975.

———. "Robert Frost: The Aesthetics of Voice and the Theory of Poetry." *Criticism* 15 (Winter 1973): 28-42.

Levinas, Emmanuel. *Existence and Existents.* Trans. Alphonso Lingis. The Hague: Martinus Nijhoff, 1978.

———. *Otherwise than Being or Beyond Essence.* Trans. Alphonso Lingis. The Hague: Martinus Nijhoff, 1981.

———. *Time and the Other.* Pittsburgh: Duquesne University Press. 1987.

———. *Totality and Infinity.* Trans. Alphonso Lingis. The Hague: Martinus Nijhoff, 1979.

Lingis, Alphonso. *The Imperative.* Bloomington: Indiana University Press, 1998.

———. *Dangerous Emotions.* Berkeley: University of California Press, 2000.

Merleau-Ponty, Maurice. *Phenomenology of Perception.* Trans. Colin Smith. London: Routledge and Kegan Paul, 1962.

———. *The Visible and the Invisible.* Ed. Claude Lefort. Trans. Alphonso Lingis. Evanston: Northwestern University Press, 1968.

Miller, David L. "Dominion of the Eye in Frost." *Robert Frost: Centennial Essays II.* Ed. Jac Tharpe. Jackson: University of Mississippi, 1976.

Miller, Lewis H. "The Poet as Swinger: Fact and Fancy in Robert Frost: *Criticism* 16 (Winter 1974): 58-72.

Miller, Perry. *The Life of the Mind in America.* New York: Harcourt, 1965.

———. *The New England Mind: The Seventeenth Century.* New York: Macmillan, 1939; Harvard University Press, 1954.

Montgomery, Marion. "Robert Frost: One Who Shrewdly Pretends." *Robert Frost: Centennial Essays II.* Ed. Jac Tharpe, Jackson: University Press of Mississippi, 1976.

Pater, Walter. *Selected Essays.* Ed. Harold Bloom. New York: New American Library, 1974.

Pearson, Keith Ansell. *Germinal Life: The Difference and Repetition of Deleuze.* London and New York: Routledge, 1999.

Peters, Robert. "The Truth of Frost's 'Directive,'" *Modern Language Notes* 75 (Jan. 1966): 29-32.

Poirier, Richard. *Robert Frost: The Work of Knowing.* New York: Oxford University Press, 1977.

———. "Frost, Burke, Winnicott." *Raritan II,* no. 2 (Fall 1982): 114-27.

Richardson, Mark. *The Ordeal of Robert Frost: The Poet and His Poetics.* Urbana: University of Illinois Press, 1997.

Rorty, Richard. *Consequences of Pragmatism.* Minneapolis: University of Minnesota Press, 1982.

———. *Philosophy and the Mirror of Nature.* Princeton, N.J.: Princeton University Press, 1980.

Rossetti, Dante Gabriel. *Collected Writings.* Selected and Edited by Jan Marsh. Chicago: New Amsterdam Books, 2000.

Thoreau, Henry David. *The Illustrated "Maine Woods."* Ed. Joseph J. Moldenhauer. Princeton: Princeton University Press, 1974.

Valéry, Paul. *The Art of Poetry*. Trans. Denise Folliot. New York: Vintage, 1958.

———. *Paul Valéry: An Anthology*. Selected, with an Introduction by James R. Lawler. Princeton: Princeton University Press, 1977.

Vendler, Helen. *The Odes of John Keats*. Cambridge: The Belknap Press of Harvard University Press, 1983.

Warren, Robert Penn. "The Themes of Robert Frost." *Selected Essays*. New York: Random House, 1958.

Wasserman, Earl R. *The Finer Tone: Keats' Major Poems*. Baltimore: Johns Hopkins Press, 1953.

Williams, William Carlos. *The Collected Earlier Poems*. New York: New Directions, 1966.

Winnicott, D. W. *The Maturational Process and the Facilitating Environment: Studies in the Theory of Emotional Development*. New York: International Universities Press, 1974.

———. *Playing and Reality*. London: Tavistock, 1971.

Winters, Yvor. "Robert Frost: or, the Spiritual Drifter as Poet." *Sewanee Review* 56 (Aug. 1948): 564-96.

INDEX OF POEMS DISCUSSED

www.ingramcontent.com/pod-product-compliance
Lightning Source LLC
Chambersburg PA
CBHW050940050726
47592CB00007B/2369